The New Man

CHRISTIANITY AND MAN'S COMING OF AGE

The New Man

CHRISTIANITY AND MAN'S COMING OF AGE

Ronald Gregor Smith

*

The Alexander Love Lectures
1955

SCM PRESS LTD
56 BLOOMSBURY STREET
LONDON

First published 1956

BT701
S57

Made and printed in Great Britain by
W. & J. Mackay & Co. Ltd., Chatham

To Käthe

CONTENTS

PREFACE

THESE lectures, the Alexander Love Lectures for 1955, were given at the invitation of the Senatus of the Theological Hall, Ormond College, Melbourne, to celebrate the ninetieth session of the Hall. The Faculty of Theology of the University of Otago also invited me to deliver a shortened version, in April 1955, at Knox College, Dunedin. In venturing to publish them, practically as delivered, I am chiefly anxious to express my gratitude to those who honoured me with these invitations, listened to me with such patience, and welcomed me so kindly into their midst—in particular Principal Hector Maclean and my old friend Professor Davis McCaughey, of Ormond College. But to them and to my other kind hosts no blame may be attached for any eccentricities in my argument.

R.G.S.

1

BIBLICAL FOUNDATIONS

In choosing as my title for these lectures *The New Man*, I felt it necessary to add a sub-title, 'Christianity and Man's Coming of Age'. I do not intend to give you now an extensive forward look over the themes of all the lectures. I can however say this much: on the groundwork of this first lecture, which is a study of the biblical teaching about the main content of the religion of Israel, I shall then attempt to present a view of the Christian understanding of man in history which, if it is acceptable, is bound to have certain important consequences for the practical matter of becoming a Christian and of the relation of Christianity to the world—for what are known currently as problems of evangelism and communication. But I must warn you that I only touch lightly on these practical matters, and am content to establish my argument on a mainly historical assessment of the problems, the successes and failures of Christianity in tackling its main task.

I think it may be of some help to you, as it certainly is to me, if I begin by taking you behind the scenes, and into the rather complicated story of the preparations

I have made for these lectures. A good many years ago now, even before I began to work as a publisher of other men's works, I had begun to collect, mainly for my own interest and edification, stories and studies of what I called to myself an anthology of conversion. I wanted to see what had really happened in the lives of men and women who had left some account of their Christian life, and especially of their entry into it. Before very long I became aware that a certain pattern, or conviction of my own about a certain similarity, was beginning to emerge, which lifted my ideas above those of any kind of psychological or hagiographical interest. Above, too, any interest which I might have had in any possible mystical change in the substance of these people's lives. Rather, I began to see that the broad similarity between, say, the life of St Augustine and the life of John Wesley was that their interests, their thought and their energy came at their conversion to be gathered up, concentrated, and then to move in a new direction, into a new life which involved nevertheless more than just a moral change, though it usually included a moral change. I found myself forced to the conclusion that these lives could only be understood properly in terms of something that was not themselves, and not even their achievement, but something objective and solid, which I ended by calling a structure of grace. They were embedded in a new ground, they were entangled in a new web, a community of relations which gave all that they did and were a new meaning.

But when I had got thus far, I found a severer problem arising. Though I could see these great figures of Christian history rising up like shining mountain peaks above the general level of Christian life, and drawing with them their friends and followers in a series of as it were secondary and anonymous conversions, there was still something strange, and inexplicable, almost fantastic, about the nature of their relation to the society round about them. Why should it be, for instance, that Augustine's conversion could usher in a change in life and direction for a whole empire, while Wesley's work should be confined to a section of one or two countries, and even there to a realm of feeling and action which can legitimately be described as individualist, emotional, and romantic? And if we were to contrast Augustine with say, Messrs Moody and Sankey, or with Dr Billy Graham of North Carolina, then the effort to subsume them all under the one category of conversion becomes almost ludicrous.

In fact, the ulterior distinction which really makes the difference lies in the presupposition which each has of man himself. It is in their understanding of what man is, in their anthropology, explicit or unconscious, that the real distinction between all these various Christian figures is to be found. To take an example from ordinary history, the example of Napoleon, it is clear that what a powerful historical figure is able to achieve depends upon what he understands man to be. It depends upon his view of the possibilities

in man. Napoleon looked upon other people as so
many things to be used, as servants for his particular
cause, and as links in the ring of adoration which he con-
trived around himself. It is not surprising that in the
end he himself was treated in the same way. He had
already removed himself from the world of human relations before he was in fact removed; he ended in an
isolation which was already real before he was forcibly
put away. Or again, if you regard man as being con-
stituted chiefly of a tangle of emotions which require
only to be sorted out and purified, then, when you
have done that, there is nothing more to be done. You
may have sorted a man out in this way in his separate
self, but you will not have begun to tackle the problem
of men living together. If you do not see man as living
first of all in the structure of unredeemed society, you
cannot be expected to bring him—or rather show him
the way, guide him—into the structure of redeemed
society, the structure of grace. What is achieved when
you are dealing with living human beings depends on
what you think it is possible for them to achieve.

This problem of a balanced and full doctrine of man
lies in the background of all that I shall try to say in
these lectures. What do we really mean when we
applaud an effort at evangelism? What do we mean
by becoming a Christian? If we put our sights high,
and refuse to be satisfied with anything less than a
total view of Christian possibilities, then the question
is not so easily answered. For the disturbing thing
about the course of Christianity through the centuries

is that it is able to lose its sense of its own immense possibilities, and to run through shallow and choked channels without being conscious of the fateful contrast with other ages. I should say that today is one of these times. The vast body of Christian people throughout the world are suffering from an eclipse; they do not see the sun, they walk in shadows, and have almost forgotten what it is like to live in the full splendour of the light. To say that they are suffering from an eclipse means that between God and them something has interposed. It is really God who is in eclipse. This something which has interposed is a false understanding of man and a false understanding of history. In such a situation, before we have any right to cry out and to search for means for a revival, we have to attempt to remove the false understanding. We must sweep and garnish, even though we have such good authority for seeing the danger that a critical standpoint may never emerge into the realm of positive movement at all.

We must first try to see what the Bible, taken as a whole and in some particular examples, has to tell us about the possibilities for man. I shall first outline a few fairly generally recognized truths, which taken together may lead us farther.

(1) The first clear assumption in the whole body of the biblical writings is that we are dealing here with history. This applies to the whole of the Bible, and not just to the so-called historical writings in the Old Testament and the Gospels and Acts in the New. It is

history in a quite particularized sense : in the career of
the tribe or a leader, in the related incidents through
the narrowly historical writings and in the reflections
upon them in the Psalms and elsewhere, clearly in the
prophetic writings, but even in the dramatic and poetic
books as well, we have to do with a quite definite
apprehension of situations and happenings within a
historical view of life. All the incidents and situations
which compose the raw material of the biblical writings arise out of the common experiences of men in
society—experiences of love and hate, of loyalty and
betrayal, of greed and self-sacrifice, of guilt and re-
stitution, of patriotism and treachery. Out of these
common experiences there rises a clear dramatic
figure, the figure of the people of Israel, one of the
two conflicting figures. But this is no pre-arranged
and static composition; Israel emerges as the chief
human figure in an unpredictable chain of events leading towards an unforeseeable conclusion. History, for
the people of Israel, is not seen as an alien force imposed upon its living situation, like the order or rule
of nature which the Greeks, for instance, were beginning to see, about the same time, as the ultimate reason by which history could be explained. But history
was forged for Israel in the living situation itself, in a
dramatic conflict of will between themselves and God.

(2) In other words, and this is the second main
truth I wish you to consider, the bewildering agglo-
meration of concrete particular situations in the Bible
is seen as having meaning which is supplied in and

through the situations themselves. The entry of God
as the other chief figure into this history is not an
extra to the history, but is the other side of the one
situation. God is not drawn in as the ultimate explanation of otherwise inexplicable happenings, say of evil
or suffering; nor is he primarily conceived, even in
the Creation stories in Genesis, as an Idea for the
satisfactory explanation of the beginning of things.
In Buber's words, 'God cannot be inferred in anything—in nature, say, as its author, or in its history
as its master, or in the subject as the self that is
thought in it. Something else is not "given" and
God then elicited from it; but God is the Being that
is directly, most nearly, and lastingly, over against us,
that may properly only be addressed, not expressed.'[1]
For Israel, God, whether as Creator or Redeemer, is
met as an active partner in each situation as it arises.
The story of the Creator at work, to take that most
extreme example, is primarily an affirmation of
personal faith in the God who created *me*; and the
story of the Redeemer is an affirmation of faith in
the personal character and permanent presence of
that same God. Each episode in the history of Israel
is the reiteration of this personal and particular relation between God and his people. There is of course
at the same time a notable awareness throughout the
Bible of the majesty and inscrutability of God; but it
is the glory and the mystery of One who is nevertheless present in the affairs of his people, and known

[1] *I and Thou*, 80–1.

B

[17]

only through this presence and in no other way. We can therefore sum up the history of the people of Israel from this standpoint as one eloquent and unceasing dialogue between the two partners, God and his people. Any more remote categories, even the later Christian modes of understanding such as those of nature and supernature, or body and soul, are foreign to the Bible.

(3) Being historical in this way, and involving this characteristic partnership between the two present elements, God and the people, the Bible has no need of recourse to subsidiary elements to reach its understanding of man. It does not indulge in subtraction or reduction from the whole situation. Neither the life of the spirit by itself, nor the development of the cultus in ritual and worship and prayer by itself, nor any kind of extraction from the living relation with God in special forms which we are accustomed to call religion —none of these things is a sufficient sphere of life for the men of the Bible. The division between the sacred and the profane—though it fights for recognition and is indeed the chief of what I should call the secondary plots in the Bible—is likewise not carried through as an autonomous explanation of human life. I find no warrant in the Old Testament, far less in the New, for that fatal distinction, which was later to petrify into a semi-permanent cleft across the whole life and thinking of the Church, for any such division of life into a sacred and a profane sphere. It is true that the New Testament, under gnostic influences, developed a con-

ception of the *kosmos*, the world, as something which stood over against God, so that in the Prologue to the Fourth Gospel we can read of the light which is God shining in the darkness of the *kosmos*. But even this distinction is not ultimate; it falls within the scope of a unified view of the world as being the created order of God. It was for all God's world that Jesus died. And the secondary developments of the distinction between sacred and profane into various realms, such as politics and economics and art and so on, which make up so large a part of our way of looking at things today, are quite foreign to the Bible view. These other interests, so far as they may be individually detected at all, are deeply embedded in the single view of Israel as living its life in the immediate presence of God. Israel is not interested in any of these things taken by itself, but in the single situation—which has, of course, different emphases at different times, but is primarily and continuously a personal situation between the two characters, Israel and God.

(4) This historical and personal view must not be confused with individualism. The relation to God is not extracted or abstracted from the history of the people; it is not an element which is isolated by the individual from the total mass. Even when the life of Israel is reduced by rebellion and exile and failure to a handful, even when it is reduced in the end to the life of the one remaining faithful one, to the Messiah on the Cross, it still remains the communal relation to God. It is a comprehensive relation which is itself a

[19]

living entity. There is no confusion of being here: God is the Creator and Israel his created people. But in this relation itself something different arises, something which is composed of the two partners and the relation as well. This is the sphere in which the new creation, the new creature, new being, is made possible. The making all things new which is the nearest to a prediction which is ever reached by the prophets, which reaches extreme forms in later apocalyptic, and reaches its glorious climax in the hope of the new age inaugurated by the Messiah, is not really a new element in the partnership of God and Israel. It is implicit in the whole historical understanding of Israel. For this newness, this new thing, is not some inexplicable, mysterious factor which might be intended to change the substance of man's being. Rather, the new thing is the working, living and being together of man and God in a relation of mutual trust and affection, what John Oman calls 'the discovery that God is worthy of trust . . . a gracious relationship which has its whole quality and distinction from being personal on both sides'[1]. It is the structure of grace which is here offered to man as his goal, not as a remote goal after the present world has passed away, but as a present element within the rebellious world, lovely and desirable as a bride, offering to man its gracious being. This is the heart of biblical eschatology—neither a final justification of history taken in the large and retrospectively, nor a completely vindicated triumph of

[1]*Grace and Personality*, 66.

superior power over a naughty world, but a present being, in the dialectic of faith even in the midst of rebellion.

(5) Lastly, in this sketchy outline of the biblical view, it is perhaps worth singling out something which I have implied in all I have said, and it is this: in their whole view of man and God the Old Testament and the New Testament are not essentially different. They compose together a unity of apprehension, a unity of history and of being which in the long run cannot be broken. Of course, there are dangers of breaks, some of them implicit in the Bible, and some of them read back into the Bible from the life of the Church, some of them even written into the New Testament by the early Church, as the form critics have shown us in recent generations. In particular the danger might be mentioned of the New Testament, with its decidedly primitive eschatology and its atmosphere of strain and even occasionally of hysteria, appearing to sanction a falling apart of the unity of history and being. Marcion is the classic example of the Christian heretic who wanted to reduce the gospel to certain limited, intense, and exclusive lines of ascetic and even gnostic theology, and to drive a wedge between the tribal God of the Old Testament and the Father-Redeemer of the New Testament. And there have been other more subtle and less easily detectable strainings of the meaning of the New Testament in the direction of a kind of religiosity, a false otherworldliness or spirituality, which are really more

dangerous because they are less obviously false, and can claim a certain justification in the New Testament itself. But here too we must hold fast to the main line, to the clear interrelation of the Old and New Testaments, indeed to the dependence of the New Testament on the Old for its whole understanding of history as a tremendous dialogue between man and God. In its firm hold on historical flesh-and-blood happenings, arising out of the passions and hopes of the men of the time, in its fulfilment of history as a dialogue between God and man, in its concern with the whole world, and in its pointing to the structure of grace as the real place of being of the community between God and the people, the New Testament is in general and in particular fulfilling the life and hope of Israel.

It is on this foundation that I should like to look briefly at one or two individual figures in the Bible to see in what respects they illustrate the truths I have just outlined. I hope that it may be possible not to lose sight of the main question about the view of man's being and the possibilities in him which can relate these things direct to our own situation.

First, I take the figure of Moses, the originator of the recognizable historical phase of Israel's life. In Ex. 3 we read how the angel of the Lord appeared to him in a flame of fire out of the midst of a bush, and how God promised to bring forth his people out of Egypt, and how God and Moses entered into a dialogue about the work Moses has to do. This is the beginning of the mighty acts of God, and it is a supremely personal encounter; the record bears, as Martin Buber says, 'a transmitted nucleus of personal experience'. But it is not personal in the sense of private or individualist. Even what are commonly called the biographical incidents are there because they lead into the real biography of Moses as it is written in the struggle of the whole people of Israel. Moses is not singled out as a personality with a religious consciousness or an interesting religious experience, but his personality and his experience are a consequence of his being singled out by God for his purpose with his people. This does not mean that the personal quality is blurred, or that Moses has to be explained away as a legendary or mythological character. But the outlines are firm and clear, they are to be seen in the objective lines of Israel's history. The total and inclusive relation of Israel to God is established by Moses in his personal experience, certainly; but it flows out from him in corporate action and corporate responsibility in such a way that it cannot be distinguished from the experience of the community. The conversion of Moses, his entry into the firm world of grace, is perhaps the mightiest event of history before Christ. Human history is made when God says to Moses, 'I will be with thy mouth, and with his [Aaron's] mouth, and will teach you what you shall do' (Ex. 4.15.)

The conversion of Jeremiah, as described in the first

chapter of the Book of Jeremiah, illustrates another
important side of the actual course of history. There is
the same threefold element, the personal meeting, the
corporate responsibility, and the unified relation with
God, as we find in all the critical encounters in the
Old Testament. But there is another element—what I
should call the element of fully-stretched normality: a
solemn dialogue, certainly, yet taking place in an
almost matter-of-fact way, unexalted and restrained.
Without ecstasy or rapture, without any division in
his life, Jeremiah obeyed the call of God, and followed
it out in sober recognition of God's concern with the
ordinary life of Israel, grounded in the policies and
passions of their everyday existence. It is not so much
that the ordinary moment was hallowed by this encounter, as that its fullest normality was found to contain already the elements of a real future for Jeremiah
and for Israel. It is here the normal man who is being
summoned, commissioned, empowered, made ready.
This moment was for Jeremiah entry into the fullest
normality of human life. That it led to solitariness,
and charges of eccentricity and even of high treason,
does not alter the fact that it was Jeremiah who saw
the inner course and meaning of the history of his
time, and brought it into the clear burning light of
God's judgment.

Lastly, I want to venture to discuss the conversion
of St Paul, as the critical element in his whole life, and
therefore, of course, in the whole movement of history
since his time. I crave your pardon for trying to do

this in a summary way. But I remind you that what we hope to recapture here is no more than the broad outline of the biblical foundations.

In St Paul we see the highest reach possible to the understanding of God and man within the context of history. For here the element in which they meet, the historical situation, has been sharpened to an almost intolerable point. For St Paul history has been fulfilled in the coming of the Messiah. Moreover, this is not an isolated occurrence. Just as in itself, in the nature of the disclosure, there can be no talk of a bolt from the blue, or an overwhelming manifestation of transcendent majesty, so in the wider historical context the coming of the Messiah is part of a close web of historical circumstances whose texture cannot be torn apart. In this situation Paul's own character and personality are not the central factor. In fact, we are not invited to be curious about the psychological elements in his make-up. The centre of his story lies elsewhere—in the web of grace in which he is caught, in the history which he now sees as completed, in the work which nevertheless remains to be done, as he presses on to the goal which has already been established for the whole of history in that same divine self-disclosure.

But though we must speak of God's work, God's action and disclosure, we must not make the mistake of deducing from this a doctrine of other-worldliness with the aim of exalting the wonder of God's action. For this web of grace which is the work

of God has been spun in the very substance of human
history—in the dim but mighty figure of Abraham
going forth without knowing whither, in Moses and
the escape from Egypt, and in the whole age-old pre-
paration of Israel. The concrete particularity and historicity of the life of the Incarnate Word, both in himself, and in his background, could not be more striking
and clear. And St Paul's personal reaction to this event
bears out that view to the utmost possible extent. His
language in the Galatians account of his conversion is
strongly reminiscent of the account Jeremiah gives of
his conversion; and even if this were not a deliberate
reminiscence the unconscious resemblance would be
equally striking and significant. St Paul is thoroughly
aware of his heritage. It is a common fallacy of exege-
sis to make use of the radical break between his pre-
conversion and his post-conversion life as a kind of
wedge driven between the Christian life and life under
the law. It is almost as common a fallacy to labour the
opposite view, and to see so many psychological preparations in St Paul's subconscious life for the break,
that in the end the break is smoothed over, and nothing startling or wonderful is left. The truth lies in a
proper balancing of the past with the new life, in understanding that crucial moment of becoming a
Christian. The difference between the old Saul and
the new Paul is indeed decisive. Paul shows as clearly
as possible a cataclysmic break with his former
actions. But he still looks at life with the same abilities
and emotional constitution, and with the same back-

ground. He was drenched in the Old Testament, the Old Testament was in the very substance and structure of his life, so that it could never be rooted out and destroyed. So he does not look back with shame on that period in his life in which he 'advanced in the Jews' religion' beyond most men of his time, 'being more exceedingly zealous for the traditions' of his fathers, as though it were a time in which he was sunk in guilt; but he looks to it rather with pride—'as touching the righteousness which is in the law, found blameless' (Phil. 3.6). In entering into Christian faith, he has, in Bultmann's words, 'not been freed from a burden, but he has brought the sacrifice of a proud past'.[1] Not even his persecution of the Church can be called a burden on his conscience, but it has rather become an occasion for the contemplation of the grace of God. 'But by the grace of God I am what I am, and his grace toward me was not in vain' (I Cor. 15. 9f.). His conversion is not liberation from frenzy, or from a false idea of God. The law does not cease to be part of revelation, but remains God's command, and full of significance and power to lead up to the time of fulfilment (Gal. 3. 23ff.). For St Paul, therefore, the revelation of Christ is the culminating stroke in a lifetime of obedience to God. His new faith in Christ does not mean the discarding of the past, but, again in Bultmann's words, 'the resolute yielding of man's self-pride, his "boasting". His conversion was

[1] *Religion in Geschichte und Gegenwart*, 2nd ed., 1930, art. 'Paulus', IV 1022.

therefore the decision to yield his whole self-understanding as it had been till that time, and to understand his existence afresh.'[1] In this revelation Paul
saw his own and Israel's understanding of man as
these were now judged by the Cross. In his response
he entered into a new being. The old life was not lost,
but gathered up into the full stretch of the finished
web of grace. This grace was not for Paul a casual de-
light like a refreshing summer shower; but it was the
very life-blood of human history, and the means by
which the whole of life was to be understood. In its
strength he established in classic form the idea of self-
hood, of personal life, in unheard-of depth and rich-
ness. But both his inner grasp and his outward look did
not turn him in on himself, but always out into the
community, into the new life which was now trium-
phantly planted in the very centre of time and space,
in the actual situation and condition of men in history.

*

Let me now try to recapitulate what I have said. In
the context of the Bible we find a remarkable conjunction of belief in a transcendent God with the significance of the actual history of the people of Israel. The
transcendence is not acquired or possessed by Israel
as an addendum to this history, it is not excogitated
from the events in such a way as to leave the events
behind; nor is it imposed upon the events in such a
way as to exalt the transcendence at the expense of

[1]*loc. cit.*

the reality of the events. But the two are woven together in an inextricable web which is itself the one
single reality for Israel. Their history is their relation
with God; and God is their history. Even in the
highest flights of the psalmists and the prophets the
holy and majestic Creator is all the time the One
who is known by his mighty acts towards and with
and in the life of Israel. We find here, therefore,
an affirmation of man and his history which is so
positive and so particularized that at first glance
it might almost seem naïve. Nevertheless, when we
look at some of the characteristic figures of that
history, it is not naïvety, but rather the subtlety
and complexity of their lives which strikes us. These
men of the Bible were able to effect a grasp on the
potentialities of their people in such a way as has not
really been repeated. They launched all the force of
their convictions in the direction of that hidden yet
most real world, that structure of grace which pene-
trates the whole of history, and so disclosed and drew
out the meaning which lies in the simplest happening.
There was in their life and understanding of human
possibilities no dissipation of enterprises: everything
was God's, everything served God, God served
everything, the whole world was a single and unique
manifestation of God's glory. In this way the possibilities of human history were infinite, for they were
the whole possibilities of God. The expectation of
Israel was for the Presence of God of which at the
same time they were already sure. In this sureness the

eschatological hope of the Bible was already proleptically actively present, bending every historical
event and bringing it under the rule of God. The
history of man was sketched and completed, as it were
in miniature, in the life of Israel.

2

THE GREAT REVOLUTION

IN my first lecture I sketched the biblical foundations, both in the Old Testament and the New Testament, of the view of man and God and history which we may call the classic Christian position. Israel and the Church, as represented in the great figures of their history, are faced with an objective claim upon their lives which we can summarily describe as the will of God. But this will is not an arbitrary imposition, nor is it the expression of an unalterable fate. Rather, it is a will which makes itself known to them in the changing historical circumstances of their lives. Neither Israel nor the Church has ever had foreknowledge of God's will by means of which they might win an impregnable position above the vicissitudes of history. Professor Eichrodt of Basel, in his very valuable study *Man in the Old Testament*, sums this up well when he writes (p. 26): 'Rather, it is into the midst of history, with all its insecurity and unforeknowable possibilities, that God's will leads.' That is to say, man's destiny and man's task are seen by Israel as embedded in history and time. In the climax of Christian history which is presented in the

New Testament documents the actual events, the decisions of many men, the pressures of all kinds of converging and unrepeatable policies and passions and prejudices, are the very substance in which God's will and man's destiny become apparent. The reality of the Spirit is not found elsewhere; it is not an addition to this concatenation of events and clashing wills, it is not some regulated and orderly world, some rule of nature, or some abstract and timeless norm set above the confused and changing world of concrete, unique and individual events and situations. The basic Christian material permits of no flight from history, but it draws us back again and again to the singularity, the particularity, the temporality, in a word, the genuine historicity which is its dominant characteristic. This particularity, I repeat, is not an arbitrary matter, even though it is without regularity in the sense of a repetition which can be shown to submit to certain external or superimposed rules of moral or spiritual behaviour. It is not the particularity of a chance conspiracy of events, but it is the particularity of an encounter which is experienced situation by situation. So we may sum the matter up by saying that God is met by Israel in the depth of Israel's understanding of what happens to itself in history.

But as we advance in time and space, with the very requirements of history itself, within the disintegrating Roman empire, a remarkable change came about in the Christian understanding of man and his destiny. In the work of St Augustine, who was faced with the collapse alike of the classical philosophies and of the Roman *imperium*, we find adumbrated a new philosophy of empire which had as its core the Christian apprehension of man. But his work was ambiguous. Mr H. J. Blackham, in his suggestive essay *The Human Tradition* (p. 154), rightly describes Augustine as 'the father of both Catholicism and Protestantism'. For whereas Augustine spoke of the commonwealth or city of the saints as 'not of this world', at the same time he admitted that the city 'does give birth to citizens here, in whom it sojourns until the time of its reign arrives'.[1] And in fact Augustine's work provided the basis for the whole temporal and spiritual achievement of the Middle Ages. Mediaeval Christendom was founded on his twofold insight into this world as being simultaneously a ruined place, 'the hospital founded by the ruined millionaire', and the place where sojourners travelled on their way to the city of promise. Out of his work there was established the twofold possibility of preserving the secular world and of raising above and beyond it another world, the eternal *civitas*. The secular world was no longer regarded as final, but as a transient structure, the terrene city which the absolute and final realm of the eternal city both sanctioned and preserved. Augustine's was the first comprehensive effort to contrive a distinctively Christian *Weltanschauung*, and it was to be the guiding principle of European thought for a thousand years.

[1]*Civ. Dei* XV, 1.

It was Thomas Aquinas, that great doctor of the mediaeval Church, whose thought is still standard for the Roman Catholic Church, who elaborated Augustine's conception of the two cities into a metaphysical structure into which the whole of human history could be fitted. But what I should call the existential insights of Augustine—insights formed by the shattering events both of his own intellectual and spiritual life and of the empire in which he lived—were composed and solidified by Aquinas into a structure which is very different from the flexible thought of Augustine. What had arisen as a labile and almost makeshift view to deal with the actual changes within the empire which was disintegrating both politically and religiously, had now been established by the greatest of the mediaeval theologians as an essentially static metaphysical system. For, to quote Friedrich Gogarten, 'this interpretation of history as a kingdom of metaphysical essences or substances, motivated teleologically within itself and comprising the whole world within this teleology, allows no historical significance to precisely that which we regard as the historical process, namely the vital experiences of living individuals in their particular characters and responsibilities. This loses its historical significance because history anticipates it by taking place within the framework of those metaphysical essences'.[1] The events and situations of history, including the specific events of the Christian revelation as well as the whole range of

[1]*Demythologizing and History*, 23.

events in human history, were now caught up and firmly embedded in a philosophical system. From that time it was the philosophical system and not the actual world of human history which dominated the thinking of Christendom. 'Thus, for example, the life and death of the individual mediaeval man is "not *his* life and not *his* death; it is not his own but the life and death of all men, and it has meaning only if he feels himself to be a member of a community which is united by a common fate. And precisely that which seems to him to be most his own, his deepest experiences, carries his thought beyond himself, as a particular historical man, towards that which is common to all mankind . . .". Consequently, it is not the historical uniqueness of the life of each individual which constitutes the substance of this mediaeval history, but the metaphysical and general which is established in advance of the historical and particular, and from which the historical and particular alone derives a significance.'[1] For Aquinas it was the cosmic element, with its conception of the *patria* towards which the travellers, the *viatores*, moved by grace, which was in the last resort the real element; and in consequence responsible human history was in the last resort infected with unreality.[2] Supernature, not nature, eternity, not time, heaven, not earth, superhistory, not history, was the abiding reality in the metaphysic of Aquinas.

[1]Gogarten, op. cit., 23.
[2]Cf. Robert Patterson, *The Conception of God in the Philosophy of St Thomas Aquinas*, 293, 443.

[35]

This was the end of an age, rather than the beginning of a new age. It was the summation of the Christian view in a subtle but precarious amalgam with Aristotle's philosophy. It was the extreme outreach of Christianity as a metaphysical system, the supreme effort to re-state the personal and objective apprehensions of the educated Christian in terms of the Greek and the Roman heritage. Greek science and speculation, Roman practical sense for order and rule, and New Testament Christianity were combined in a single continuous metaphysical web. It is hardly possible to exaggerate the splendour and power of that achievement. This was one possible form of Christian civilization; and whatever the defects, the violence, the crudity and the uncertainty in the balance of the constituent elements, nevertheless nothing like it has ever been seen. Christianity and western culture combined with such splendid results for Christianity as well as culture that no one can look back on that time without admiration and respect. We must not allow the fear of being called sentimental or archaic to shield us from the clear view of an epoch which gave us St Francis and Dante, the cathedrals and even the crusades.

In all these historical figures and events there are still to be discerned the two sides of Augustine's thought, held together in that otherworldly hope which was really a passion rather than a hope, a passion which included this world and its affairs as well as the eternal world. Nevertheless, as I have said,

Aquinas marked an end rather than a beginning. For in his concern for the majesty of God's eternal purpose with the world he shifted the centre of gravity from this world to the next. The philosopher who began with Aristotle from human experience, who wished to 'hew his way through the senses' to the insensible world, ended by splitting life in two. The lines which he set for a Christian civilization in the end wavered and failed because in essence he did not allow proper weight to the splendour and fecundity of human enterprise and imagination of which he himself was such a notable example. The Thomist philosophy proved inadequate in its doctrine of man. In other words, Aquinas misunderstood himself. He did not see in man and human history the real clue to existence, even though in his mythology he recognized the central place of man. In Dilthey's words, 'the object of religion was characterized by the grandiose, the substantial, the eternal . . . a remarkable metaphysical coldness flows from this transcendent world'.[1] And, again in Dilthey's words, 'it was metaphysics as theology which was the real bond which in the Middle Ages held together religion, learning and art, the different sides of the intellectual and spiritual life'.[2]

Over against this metaphysical *tour de force* of the Middle Ages there arose that remarkable combination of forces which I term the Great Revolution. It is a

[1]*Auffassung und Analyse des Menschen im 15. und 16. Jahrhundert*, 19f.

[2]*Einleitung in die Geisteswissenschaften*, 365f.

revolution which has gone on till our own day. The
new world which was ushered in with the break-up of
mediaeval civilization is still our modern world; no
other great change has taken place, and in fact a proper assimilation of the change which then took place
is still our main task and way into a responsible future.
Other significant stages in modern history, such as
the Age of Enlightenment, the French Revolution,
the Industrial Revolution, the Russian Revolution,
the immense changes in our own day in the work and
self-understanding achieved by men through the
natural and humane sciences, are no more than
successive attempts to establish the means of understanding what man is, or must become, as a
consequence of the loss of the mediaeval metaphysic.

The essence of the change lay in man's self-understanding. Its common and generic name is the Renaissance, and this name indicates one at least of the
motive forces of the change: the resurgent power,
namely, of the old philosophy, the classical Greek tradition in European history. Yet, if we remember that
one of the characteristic figures of the Italian Renaissance, Petrarch, was deeply involved in his whole being in a dialogue with St Augustine, this may be taken
as a sign of the truth that the break through of the human spirit at the Renaissance cannot be simply
ascribed to the liberating influence of Greek thought.
I think it is truer to say that at the Renaissance we see,
among other things, an efflorescence of the Christian
spirit which went beyond the bounds prescribed by

mediaeval philosophy. Of course the particulars of this change may be disputed, and it is even fashionable to question whether there was, at the close of the mediaeval epoch, any distinctive change at all. But though the chosen date and circumstances may differ in a description of the break through of the human spirit, and though its significance may be variously assessed according to the relativities of the critic's own standpoint, that such a change did take place seems to me to be one of the cardinal facts in the whole course of Christianity. Personally, I should see in the life and poetry of the troubadours the first unmistakable stirrings of that change. For in their view of life people and things became interesting, and asserted their existence, in their own right. And in due course the form of life for the people who were to become the modern European nations ceased to be held within the bonds of a metaphysical theology which had held together all the different aspects of life. But these peoples now discovered all manner of new and autonomous interests and pursuits: the religious experience of the individual, the independence of intellectual pursuits, the liberated imagination in art, the liberated individual in political organization, the rise of new political and economic groupings, the rise of politics as an independent art, and finally a new philosophy in the attitude of the experiencing subject to reality. In brief, what took place was a change in the *status hominis*, the condition of man, which was characterized by what

Dilthey calls 'free manifoldness' in his view of the world. The old metaphysics was simply unable to cope with this situation, and since that time metaphysics has no longer been able, in the guise of theology, to make good its claim to be the queen of the sciences. Since that time metaphysical systems have simply been in competition with one another, and with other ways of looking at man and the world, in such a way that it is clear that they have become private matters, optional systems, and can no longer claim to be the crown of human existence.[1]

The change was in man's self-understanding. That is to say, the change lay within his understanding of history. History was no longer seen as the necessary but tiresome ante-chamber of supra-history, but as an existent power whose meaning could be sought in itself. This was the fundamental insight which broke the bonds of mediaeval metaphysics, and with it the very structure of mediaeval civilization. Out of this has flowed the work of the natural sciences from Francis Bacon to Heisenberg, of literature from Shakespeare to Mr Eliot, of historical criticism from Lessing to Bultmann, of modern philosophy from Giordano Bruno to the philosophers of linguistic analysis, of political science from Machiavelli to Lenin—and indeed of every sphere over which human activity has ranged and flowered in the last five hundred years. All this activity was possible because man understood his situation in history in a new way.

[1] Cf. Dilthey, *Einleitung*, 356f.

He saw himself as free, and as responsible for making his own life, and as open to a future which was not an arbitrary or threatening disposition of fate, but was awaiting him as his own destiny. History came to be seen as the way in which man understood his own being as the free and responsible climax to his given situation.

If I may cite just one example of the amazing efflorescence of the human spirit at the beginning of the modern epoch, then perhaps the words of Luther in his *Address to the German Nobility* are the most revealing and instructive. Though Luther himself is an ambiguous figure, whose course through history prepared the way for a new metaphysical theology almost as much as it liberated the forces of humanity in the Great Revolution, there can be no serious opposition to the claim that he towers above his contemporaries and succeeding generations in his strong grasp both of the historicity of Christian faith and of the detailed working out of it in every area of human life. The words I wish to quote are simply these: 'The sphere of faith's works is worldly society and its order'. As Dilthey says, justly, 'With this sentence there enters into history one of the greatest organizing thoughts that a man has ever had'.[1]

'The city of God', said Augustine, 'gives birth to citizens here'. Augustine's other side, this descriptive and liberating side of his Christian apprehension, was taken up explicitly by Luther, and implicitly by the

[1] *Auffassung*, 61.

whole of the modern world, and used as a weapon against the metaphysical activity of the Middle Ages. From that time the concern of men has been with the realities of human history as containing their own principles of movement and explanation, and their own clear and self-authenticating autonomy from any kind of metaphysical system, and even from one another. The confusion into which society was thereby cast at that time has not yet been resolved; but it is important to note that it is a confusion arising out of a positive insight into the significance of man's life in history, which was gained in open conflict with the mediaeval insistence on an over-arching supra-historical concept of life which could no longer support the pressure of human demands.

It is important, therefore, to note that this revolution in human self-understanding is not in its essence at variance with Christianity. Its fundamental element is the decision to take the history of man as the controlling material for an understanding of man's destiny. The men of the Renaissance were too thoroughly versed in mediaeval thought to propose any cheap kind of secondary humanism as the solution to the impasse in which they speedily found themselves. So when Luther spoke of 'worldly society and its order' as the sphere of faith's activity, he was of course speaking in the first place negatively and controversially, against the mediaeval conception of otherworldliness which placed redemption beyond the policies and responsibilities of history. But he was also speaking

positively, in terms of his understanding first of the
whole biblical view of man and second and in particular of the meaning of the Incarnation. And this indeed
seems to me to be one inescapable consequence of any
doctrine of the Incarnation, of God becoming man,
namely, that man in history is the important matter.
The concern of the patristic and mediaeval theologians with the effect of their inherited Greek philosophy upon this doctrine leaves untouched the awe-
inspiring simplicity and audacity of the belief itself. It
was this belief which Luther saw afresh as an affirmation of man's destiny in history, in whose strength he
was able to waken the dormant vigour of Christian
faith and sweep it into fresh channels. The multitudinous speculations about the nature of transcendence and eternity, and their relation to immanence and
time, which had arisen in the philosophical struggles
of the Fathers and the early Councils, were not without their grandeur, or their political and historical
significance at a certain remove. But in the outflow of
the Renaissance in that particular channel which we
call the Reformation those speculations gave way before the primary affirmation of man's destiny in this
world. The cosmos, instead of being regarded as a
rigid abstraction superimposed on history, was seen
again in its Hebrew sense as the creation which God
wished to redeem; and this creation, in its chief manifestation, is the world where man plays his part.

This primary emphasis at the Renaissance, this re-
covery of Hebrew this-worldliness, was of course not

merely and not simply a theological insight. It included other elements, and it was obscured by the
very fluidity of the historical situation itself. Nevertheless, it has been the dominant element in the history of civilization since that time. It involved the
abandonment of the idea of Christianity as providing a
religious superstructure for human life and history;
and at the same time it brought Christian faith into an
intense twofold relation to human history. Christianity was no longer seen as being primarily a religion about another world; indeed, it was no longer
seen as a religion at all, comparable with the other
religions which imposed standards and norms upon
society. But it was seen to be in the very substance of
society, both as a critical dissolvent element and as
the very means by which society could understand
itself. That is to say, it was on the one hand critical,
in that everything in society came under the judgment
of the Word of God as accomplished and fulfilled in
time and history. Human culture was seen (for instance, by Calvin) as ridden with sin and imperfection.
But on the other hand this critical element was accom-
panied by a positive and hopeful element: in the
strength of that same Word, the God-man who had
honoured human life, the same human society was
offered, as symbolically in those words of Luther's,
its only ground of hope. 'Worldly society and its
order' needed to be purified and changed; but it
was no longer seen as merely the shadowy corridor
leading to the real world of light. For this human

society was the place where God had chosen to work out human destiny. Here and nowhere else, here where ruin was brought upon man by his own irresponsibility, the reconstruction was to take place. So the division between the sacred and the profane was removed, the distinction between the religious and the secular, the difference between the shepherds and the sheep. Nothing was sacrosanct any more. The Old Testament and New Testament insight into the integrity of human life was recovered. Human life involved not two worlds, but one world; not a two-fold system with nature and super-nature neatly dovetailed into one another, but one world, into which God's Word penetrated. Not a world of the hierarchy and a world of ordinary men, not a world of honours students and pass students, but a single cosmos.

But one signal difference from the Hebrew view of man and the world appeared with the Renaissance. The extraordinary effort required to throw off the incubus of mediaeval metaphysical dualism led to an extraordinary emphasis on the autonomy of man. The unity and integrity of man and the cosmos were seen as permitting, indeed demanding, an independent development of manifoldness, of multitudinous enterprises with their own terms of reference and principles of movement. The strict subsumption of all enterprises under the aegis of the Creator-Redeemer which we find in the Old Testament, and also, though less clearly, in the New Testament, was no longer taken as a matter of course. In the overriding, overruling strength of the trust and honour which were placed in the human creation by the very fact of the Incarnation, free play was given to human enterprises of the most diverse kinds. Nothing was seen as religious any more, because everything came under the fruitful and liberating impulse of the Word made flesh. Everything was now related, not to a metaphysical order which imposed degrees and stations of reality upon creation, but to the hope of the fulfilment of human destiny in the strength of the Word who had come and would come again.

In other words, society at the Renaissance did not become pagan, but truly human, because eschatological. By this I mean that God was not lost to the men of the Renaissance. His place in a mythological universe and a metaphysical system was certainly abandoned—not all at once, of course, but in principle as soon as the critical sciences, of history and literature and later of the natural sciences, got under way, and as soon as political science was able to develop a doctrine of the autonomous leaders of history which would enable a man like David Friedrich Strauss, for instance (true child of the Renaissance) to speak of God as no longer having any fixed address or occupation. But this does not mean that God was lost. Rather, he was encountered in many fresh places and ways within history itself. Panentheism, romanticism, idealism, moralism of one kind and another have sought to elicit the truth about God's loss of a home over against the world; or more precisely, these varying philosophies and attitudes have tried to explain man's changed position in a world where God had lost his old mythological and metaphysical status. While none of these views has proved satisfactory in the long run—mainly because they have all succumbed to one form or the other of a mythological or a metaphysical absolutism which was in fact no longer tenable as a presupposition of thought—nevertheless, it is important to see that all such efforts have in common an eschatological insight which is not of the old metaphysical kind. The eschatological impulse which filled them was no longer the abstract hope of some kind of supra-historical (that is, non-historical) conclusion to the whole of history; but it was a living insight into the present condition of man in history as containing in itself the meaning of history. I do not mean by this a kind of completely realized eschatology, brought directly into the sphere of history by the sheer fact of the Incarnation; but rather I mean an eschatology which, while it contains the historical Word in itself as its triumphant exemplar, has also other moments, figures, situations, in which that same Word recurs in exemplary and dynamic fashion. It is no honour to the uniqueness of the Incarnate Word to set him in such lonely separation from the embarrassments of history that he is left high and dry in a docetic desert, or swinging in ineffectual space, high in some mythological heaven. The right hand of God is here in the life of man in history, and this is where the

Word may be encountered. The Word is as continuous, sustained and dominant in history as God himself. Nor is it sufficient to interpose here a separated doctrine of the Holy Spirit as being the continuous and creative activity of God in history. For the question of the significance of the Incarnate Word can only be answered in terms of continuing pressure, of dialogue in the situations of history. It is in this sense that the Renaissance, which undoubtedly disembarrassed God of his metaphysical and mythological trappings, did not really lose God. Even a man like Nietzsche, who could say 'God is dead', was not so much denying the reality of God as abusing the unreality which had by his time usurped the name of God.

The Renaissance, then, found a fresh impulse for historical activity in a fresh understanding of humanity. It found this fresh understanding in the New Testament conception of the world as one, as alienated, indeed, from God, yet with the possibility of being turned again to God in the strength of God's own initiative of trust in it. So the idea re-entered human history that God was for this world, for man, at the same time as he was against it in its aspect of closed self-sufficiency. Society received the double gift of hope and judgment: men were able to hope in their own future to unimaginable limits, and at the same time were given the weapon of God's understanding of humanity as a means of self-criticism and condemnation. This combination of positive hope with a sense of self-criticism and need of perpetual reformation was unexampled in history. In its strength men hoped for such achievements as had never before been possible. With fresh and eager curiosity men turned outwards and inwards; they sailed the seas of the world, and of their secret selves, conscious that the secrets they had still to unravel nevertheless lay within their grasp, in the one world in which they were placed. History had fully taken over; nature was but the raw material, metaphysics and a possibly more real world only a misleading dream. Man had come of age.

It was to be a long time before this maturity of man was properly acknowledged. To this day the ideas of the Renaissance have had to fight for recognition. The seed of delay and of difficulty lay in the departure from the Hebrew idea of this-worldliness, so that the implicit transcendence of that view tended to give way before a naïve immanentism. The proper and necessary autonomy of man and his pursuits tended to become a closed and self-sufficient autonomy. The splendid and fruitful dialectic of a this-worldly transcendence which is at the heart of the Hebrew view was not sustained. The promised fulfilment did not come. The foretaste of true historical life, given in miniature in the life of Israel, was held up before men once more. But it was no more than a foretaste. The banquet itself has still to be spread. The world has still to take to itself the whole gospel in the fullness of its historical hope.

3

DEADLOCK

I N my last lecture I described the Great Revolution
which took place at the Renaissance in man's view
of himself in history, which I ended by calling
man's coming of age. A significant opportunity was
opened up for Christianity not only to free itself from
the bonds of a dualistic metaphysics but also to enter
on a new course in relation to its understanding of
God and of the world and of man's historical destiny.
In the outflow of spiritual and intellectual and physical energy into a truly breath-taking variety of enterprises, it was possible, and for a time seemed prob-
able, that at the centre of this outreaching of the human spirit the energy of Christianity would be the cor-
rective and shaping element, guiding the autonomous
enterprises, penetrating them, and in turn being penetrated by them. It seemed as though it were indeed
possible for a new kind of civilization to arise, which
could develop, in unheard-of depth and grandeur,
what Professor Tillich would call a theonomous life.
By a theonomy Tillich means, to use his own words, a
'culture expressing in its creations an ultimate con-

cern and a transcending meaning not as something strange but as its own spiritual ground. "Religion is the substance of culture and culture the form of religion".[1]

But this possibility has not so far been fulfilled. What happened, in the confusion of interests and possibilities which succeeded the break-up of the mediaeval heteronomous culture was that—speaking in broad outline—the Church and civilization went separate ways. Western society broke up not only into a great number of more or less independent nation-states, with almost unlimited ambitions of self-assertion and self-aggrandizement; but its cultural interests also developed in a multitude of independent ways. These ambitions and interests were based on a conception of the unfettered autonomous human spirit of exploration and inquiry which was bound by nothing save the consideration of the 'given facts'. Human life was seen as an autonomous entity, which could be understood and controlled in terms of principles derived not from outside itself, but always from within its own history. To quote Tillich again, 'autonomy is the dynamic principle of history . . . (it) is not necessarily a turning-away from the unconditional. It is, so to speak, the obedient acceptance of the unconditional character of the form, the logos, the universal reason in world and mind. It is the acceptance of the norms of truth and justice, of order and beauty, of personality and community. It is

[1] *The Protestant Era*, 36.

obedience to the principles that control the realms of individual and social culture'.[1] The old categories of body and spirit, nature and super-nature, profane and sacred, no longer played the chief controlling part. These categories were derived from the metaphysical heteronomy of the late Middle Ages, and gave way before the category of history as 'the outstanding category of interpreting reality'.[2] In this new historical autonomy the distinguishing categories were found within the integral life of man, that is, man's life seen as a single whole, an independent entity. The divisions now run through man and his history and no longer through man and God, earth and heaven. From this new maturity of man in history there have flowed all the characteristically modern developments: historical science, archaeology, economics, politics, psychology, sociology, and the natural sciences—all resting, whatever their differences and even conflicts of interest, on the same ground of man's nature regarded as an autonomous entity. The fruits of this maturity have been exhilarating as well as frightening. But our present fears should not blind us to the immense gains which have thereby been made available for western civilization, and through it for the whole world. As Cyprian said of the Church during the decay of the Roman empire that 'it stands upright among the ruins', so we must also acknowledge that in the ruins of the great Christian experiment of the Middle Ages, man him-

[1]Op. cit., 52.
[2]Op. cit., 30.

self stood upright, and took over his own rule without fear.

Against this autonomous development, this conception, commonly called secular, of man and his destiny, the Church reacted slowly, but powerfully and in the end without many signs of regret or attempt at conciliation. While the activist humanist Renaissance gradually developed its resources, opening up one field after another to its open-minded curiosity about the 'facts', the Church drew slowly back within itself, reiterating what seemed to it to be the 'essential facts'. The situation was not essentially different in the Protestant churches and in the rump of the old Church, though on the whole the Protestant churches have in the course of these centuries shown more clearly both their close affinity to and appreciation of the new civilization of autonomous humanism, or historism, as I should prefer to call it, and the violence of reaction against it. The Roman Church has maintained a much more even keel, relying consistently on its heteronomous attitude, with its unbroken tradition and claim of continuous authority. In the Protestant world there have been both conflicts and attempts at accommodation, as one strongpoint after another was attacked by the spirit of autonomous man. The prolonged and bitter controversy in the eighteenth century between the *illuminati* and the evangelical party in England, which was mostly regarded as a quarrel about the evidence of the gospel miracles for the truth of Christianity, was in fact one of the crucial points at

which the Church's conception of the authority of revelation had to yield before the onslaught of the conception of autonomous human reason. In this conflict
David Hume played a conspicuous part whose importance has been increasingly recognized. Nothing less
than two ways of understanding human existence
came into conflict, and in the sharpness of that controversy and its succeeding phases in the nineteenth
and twentieth centuries, the separation of ways became increasingly clear.

The conflict affected both sides, but it has been, I
believe, the Church which has suffered most. For the
perennial temptation of every religion, which seeks to
understand and explain human life in terms of some
unconditional ground, is to short-circuit the principles
controlling the individual and society by means of
principles of understanding and explanation brought
in from outside human life itself: some secure foot-
hold from which it may survey mankind, offering men
consolation and assurance, indeed, but at the same
time making it a condition of that offer that it itself,
the religion, should be accepted along with these gifts,
as the purveyor of them. The Church, following this
temptation, has more and more, in recent centuries,
sharpened and strengthened its understanding of its
message conceived as a separate instrument of power.
It has attempted to contrive for itself, out of the fragments of the whole tradition of Christian authority, a
new heteronomous structure. The orthodox elaboration of creeds, confessions, catechisms, liturgies and

rituals—and now, in our time, of a new insistence on what is called biblical theology—may be summarily described as a series of attempts to build up a structure of authority to replace the broken tradition of the mediaeval Church. But all this effort betrays a fundamental difference from the early history of the Church. Then the fundamental concern was to express— through the exigencies of conflict with heretics and unbelievers, certainly, but still, simply to express— unconditional concern for the historical needs of men. Since the coming of age of man in society, however, the fundamental concern has changed: the Church has sought to *preserve* its message, and with the message to preserve itself. It has sought to do this by imposing itself and its message as an alien law on man's mind. It has sought to define this task, and its whole situation vis-à-vis society, in terms of delimitation of interests. Then it has proceeded to aim at exercising power on society by the establishment of its heteronomous authority.

Let me pause a moment, to make clear what I mean by this word: following Tillich's fruitful terminology, I mean by a heteronomy a system of ideas, or a structure of laws, which seek to impose themselves on the forms of a society to which they are fundamentally alien. Heteronomy 'disregards the logos structure of mind and world. It destroys the honesty of truth and the dignity of the moral personality. It undermines creativity and the humanity of man. Its symbol is the "terror" exercised by absolute churches or absolute

states.'[1] A very good example of a heteronomous
church and state in unholy alliance was the action of
the magistrates of Edinburgh for some time during
the eighteenth century. Acting on the advice of the
presbytery of the church, the magistrates appointed
two baillies or baillifs to parade the streets of Edinburgh during the hours of church service, with power
to arrest and fine any citizens who were found pro-
menading instead of being in church. But there are
many examples, for which we do not really need to
cast back into other centuries. A heteronomous authority, especially a church, is not willing to allow the
world to be itself, not even when that world is a mature world with its own forms and purposes, not even
when that world has derived its fundamental impulse
and its historical self-understanding from the very
heart and substance of Christian faith itself—as our
modern world has done. This heteronomous effort
reaches a typical climax in the modern orthodoxy or
neo-orthodoxy known variously as the theology of
crisis, dialectical theology, or the theology of the
Word. I scarcely need to point out that in making this
criticism I am not decrying the magnificent power
and splendour of some of the manifestations of neo-
orthodoxy: the concern for the *kerygma*, or essential
message of the gospel, the attention to the actual history and theology of the Bible, the devotion, even the
passion, with which the omnipotence and judgment of
God are proclaimed over against all human confusion

[1]Op. cit., 52.

and distortion of revelation. Nevertheless, the question which we have to ask is whether the Church is really fulfilling in this way the fundamental concern for man and his history which is the reason for its existence. 'The Word of God is not a word spoken only to the ears, or even necessarily to the ears at all. The Word of God is his self-communication which can occur in many forms and is not bound to the human word. It may occur through actions, gestures, forms— of course, not *ex opere operato* (by their mere performance), but nevertheless without any accompanying word. Sacraments, visible symbols, bodily, musical, artistic expressions are "Word of God" even if nothing is spoken—that is, for those who accept them spiritually (as the spoken word is Word of God *only* if it is received spiritually).'[1]

We might go farther than Tillich in this, and ask whether a Church which has even such a wide and generous understanding of the context and utterance of the Word of God has found the proper relation to human life and society. For in the end the Church in its fundamental concern should not be living in a different world from the rest of men. It does not stand outside this world, it is not in heaven, it does not even carry the responsibility for heaven, that is, for God's place and power. The work which the Church does truly for God it does by being truly for men, with men, and it does this work through men. This conception of the Church's task cuts from underneath it all

[1]Tillich, op. cit., 218.

supposed security, all sacrosanct authority, all search
for a lever of power on the world, all heteronomous
ambitions. The Word of God may then be seen as
being spoken in ever new forms which are created
out of the experiences and enterprises of men in the
actual situations where they are.

But though the divergence is violent and sharp between the life of autonomous secularized man and the
would-be heteronomous life of the Church, the fundamental concern of both parties is the same: it is the
life of man. The lesson I draw from the struggle of
recent centuries is that neither party is complete without the other. The free exercise of the human spirit in
the autonomous consideration of the objects presented
to it is legitimate and right; man's relation to the objects in his world, to his own history, does contain
unconditional validity. But this validity is not
complete without the recognition of certain inescapable boundaries which lie across its path. And on
the other hand the obedient devotion of the human
spirit to the objects of Christian revelation is not complete without the recognition of the freedom of the
human spirit. The recognition of the need for obedience to bounds in the one case does not damage freedom, and the recognition of freedom in the other case
does not damage obedience. The unsolved mediaeval
controversy about the freedom or predestination of
the will cannot be solved either by the heteronomous
assertions of the post-mediaeval churches or by the
autonomous defiance of a sterile and secondary hu-

manism. To cling to either side of the controversy as giving the solution to the human predicament really means to cling to one side or the other of a metaphysical misunderstanding.

Both sides, I repeat, have in common the situation of man in history, in this one world. The struggle is round man himself, and an understanding of what he is. What we are concerned with, therefore, is the search for a new anthropology, a view of man, which will pay proper respect both to the insights of the Renaissance about man and the insights of Christianity about God in relation to man. In this search I do not believe that it can be fruitful, or even legitimate, to attempt to take our stand on the old battle-fields, where the corpses of decaying categories are locked in meaningless embrace, where revelation lies stricken beside reason, where the supernatural lies dead beside the natural, where the trumpet of the Lord, borrowed by the dying dogmatist, lies tarnished by the side of the deaf and also dying secular hero, captain of his fate no longer. The knight of faith, as Kierkegaard called him in a beautiful image, can no longer come prancing into the tournament in the panoply of absolute assurance. Absolute solicitude, yes; and absolute resignation. For he comes not from another world but in the new hope and strength which he is given in this world because of what has been done in and for this world. Like his master, he is the servant, so far as he may be, of men.

In the historical situation of man, then, it is

necessary to recognize that freedom and obedience both
have their place. The human spirit is free so far as it
knows no limits within itself to the possibilities which
it may unfold. And the human spirit is at the same
time bound to strict obedience to the facts out of
which these possibilities flow. These facts are the
given objects, the things and people, by which it tests
and develops its freedom. Everything that man under-
takes he does so in virtue of the things and people
coming towards him from outside himself. He did not
make them, he did not think of them, he did not ask
for them: they are there, in their own right of existence. Man is made by his free acceptance, in unlimited
openness, of what comes to him out of the surround-
ing darkness.

And likewise the Christian, though bound by his
special facts, what he calls the 'facts of the revelation',
and thus also, formally speaking, bound by what
comes from outside himself, by what he neither in-
vented nor imagined, is at the same time invited into
a realm of freedom. Admittedly, if we limit our gaze
simply to the historical manifestations of Christianity,
we are at once involved in all manner of fateful and
even baleful circumscriptions of this realm of freedom.
Throughout its history the Church has struggled with
the invitation to freedom as though it were an incubus
of which it would like to be rid. Authority, and ex-
pediency, and the exercise of power by virtue of certain semi-magical delimitations of influence, have all
played an insidious part in diverting the energy of

Christendom from its proper sphere. The doctrine of
the Holy Spirit in an integral unity with a full doctrine of the Word has always been the laggard in the
armoury of Christianity. For it is in this teaching that
the explosive and revolutionary quality of Christianity is seen at its most potent: the teaching, namely,
which affirms man and his history as leading through
grace into unimagined spheres of truth and freedom.
The generally neglected teaching about freedom
which lies at the very heart of Christianity is an affirmation of man's infinite possibilities.

For it is in a proper grasp of the life of the Spirit as
actually constituting the community of Christians
that the ancient energies of Christianity may be re-
discovered. Though the tragic course of one of the
first great movements of the Spirit in the life of the
Church—the Montanist movement, which included
in its story the life of Tertullian, one of the truly
original thinkers of the Church—can scarcely now be
seen as anything but inevitable, nevertheless, it
must be said that here as elsewhere the Church has
ever been quick to protect its gains, to retain its
status as an authority in the world, and slow to see the
dialectic in its obedience to its own calling. For this
calling is not to a *position* in the world, but to a disclosure of the dialectic in man's own being, in the
heart of history: a dialectic which demands freedom
as well as obedience, absolute openness, unreserved
togetherness with others, as the very place where the
Spirit is present. God's presence is thus not a shadowy

longing in the life of the Church, but the very being
of Christianity in the world. Living with this presence
cannot be guaranteed in any due observance of the
Church's forms, or recognition of its authority, but
is to be awaited wherever men find themselves
brought together in some common purpose. The
Church as a sociological entity has no monopoly or
guarantee of the presence of the Spirit, but is on the
contrary by its very nature as an established social
institution in constant peril of losing the Spirit.

It is a feeble and insufficient recognition of the newness of the Incarnation as a given fact of the human
situation which has led the Church into its recoil from
the Renaissance. And it is the consequent reaction of
the humanists which has sharpened the division to the
point of tragedy. It is not too much to say that until
this tragic division has been overcome the modern
world is going to find no way through its deadlock.

For on the one hand, among the unchurched humanists, though truth has been the guiding star, the
recognition of bounds has faded. And on the other
hand in the Church, though being has been the explicit
goal, this has been sought in the strength of a false
spirituality, what Kierkegaard called religiosity, and
the search for truth has been broken off. The greatest
achievements of modern Christianity have been in the
realm of individualism, of private religion, of pietism,
while community, being together, has practically dis-
appeared. And with this loss of community individualism has replaced true being in the life of the Church,

and has ousted the hope of a proper ontology and ground for community. In recent centuries all the dangers of an unbounded search for truth, or an unbounded pursuit of being, each in separation from the other, has characterized the two parties, the humanist and the church parties. There has been an almost complete disregard of the disintegrating community which belongs to neither side of the ideological conflict, but to man, the battleground. Individualism, romanticism, subjectivism, antinomianism, licence of one kind or another, on the Christian or the humanist side, have been the accepted situation. On the Christian side these things have taken the form of sectarian or fissiparous tendencies, or the arrogant individualism of devotion to the inner light, or convulsive revivalism increasingly losing its contact with the forms of the given objects of the faith, and depending on a whipped-up concentrate of mock and archaic being— in brief, we see the loss of the object, of true transcendence, in a vain effort to achieve conversion by one's own inward powers of being. On the humanist side the devotion to the truth of the object, without a corresponding recognition of the bounds imposed by the proper being of the object in community, that is, in its relationships with the rest of the world, has led to more and more frantic acquisition of objects of truth in separated meaninglessness. The scientists who today represent in the common view the vanguard of human enterprise are lost in a desert, each in his own desert of truth.

The two sides share the one failure, the failure to recognize the union of freedom with bounds, of facts with relationships. This failure is focused in the failure to understand man himself. The Christians are lost in devotion to a false and separated Thou, not the great eternal Thou of given transcendence: and the humanists are lost in a false and separated It, not the living It by which man is able to reach the Thou, the It which may become a Thou. This is a failure in self-understanding, and the collapse of Christianity and humanism alike.

A new approach is needed: the combination of the situation with the relation, of what we are with what faces us. It is the problem of the nature of the object, the nature of the relation, and the meaning of transcendence.

The problem is not insoluble. But a prerequisite for its solution is the confession of the Church, on the one hand, that it has too long regarded the sphere of history as one which it is called to govern and control, and the readiness of the adult mature world, on the other hand, to perceive the ground of its work and hope in the same history, a history which carries with it unconditional validity.

The mysterious and crucial and unconditional moment in that history is still that point where the Christian affirmation about Christ is to be encountered. But in order to let this point of human history be effective in its own radiance it is necessary not to confuse it with the heteronomous ecclesiastical doctrines about

it, or with the sterile relativisms of unbridled humanism. The crucial problem for human life and thought
is the problem of transcendence. This is not an acade-
mic problem, it is not confined to metaphysical speculation about the limits of human thought and what lies
beyond these limits. But the problem has been set by
the Christian affirmation of the Incarnation in the
midst of human life, the same life which is shared by
the Christian and the non-Christian.

And when I say that the problem of transcendence
is in the midst of human life I am demanding from the
humanist and the Christian alike the recognition of
something that is not in the first instance a matter of
faith, and therefore a matter of response to a given
message about Christ, but simply a matter of sight, of
everyday experience. I mean, that in every human
situation there is a relation: a relation between the
tool and the user of the tool, between the object under
investigation and the investigator, between yourself
and the other person with whom you have to do. Life
is characterized by these relations. Above all in the
relation between two persons it becomes clear that
the relation is only possible because there is a difference. It is the otherness of the other which rises up
before you, in conflict or in understanding. This is the
basic manifestation of transcendence in human life.
This is what faces you in every situation into which
you enter without reserve or reduction. This otherness or transcendence is not an extra brought in from
some remote sphere of understanding, but it is the

E   [65]

central element which makes the situation, that is, the relation, the humanity of life, possible at all. An absolute solitary is not a human being.

To put the matter sharply, as sharply as possible, in terms of modern Christian dogmatics, I believe that it is meaningless to assert, over against the secularized world, that the God of the Christians is 'wholly other'. The importance of the intention behind this assertion is clear: it is the attempt to give God his glory, to preserve his otherness, to indicate his absolute difference from his creation. But it is meaningless, because an assertion about the 'wholly otherness' by its own definition excludes any relation or knowledge of what is *wholly* other. And this assertion, besides being meaningless, distorts the sense and drift of Christianity. For the otherness which we meet in God is that otherness which we are able to meet only because he has made himself present to us, has brought himself into relation with us, in all the variety of the historical situations in which each one of us is set. We know God as transcendent because we meet him as the one who fills our present. We believe him because we know him in these situations. We believe him because he has made himself known to us in history, in humanity, in Israel, and especially in the life situation of one man, in the Incarnation.

In sum, we believe in God because we meet him in the midst of history. God is not at the end of our inquiries, nor is he the stop-gap where our thoughts fail us. To treat him in this way is to betray a fundamental disbelief both in his work as Creator and his work as Redeemer. The God of Christian belief is not a *deus ex machina* who can be called in, in the name of an other-worldly hope beyond all appearances, a god whose real home is up in the clouds, or in the wings of the theatre where man's little drama is being played out. But he is in the midst of the drama, which turns out, in consequence, to be no mere spectacle, but the real thing. We are driven to this conclusion by the very affirmation of man's life and being which is presented to us in that crucial moment of human history, the Incarnation.

On this view the beginning of a new *rapprochement* between the world and the Church depends primarily on the Church's fresh understanding of its commission and its situation. The Church is not called to be the governess of a child under age, or the warder of a con-demned world. But Christians are rather placed under a double allegiance, an allegiance to the world, and an allegiance to God. In actual living history, however, this allegiance is not two things, but two sides of the one thing. For Christians in this regard as in every other cannot be more than their master, whose rela-tion to God was lived out in his relation to the world. Christ is not a heavenly fantasy, or a *tour de force* on the part of an inaccessible otherness; but he is the givenness of transcendence, he is transcendence in its only accessible form, namely, in a human life in human history, in the one world which all men share as the place of their destiny.

If this recognition were really existential in the
Church, then a great deal of contemporary ecclesiastical effort, as well as a great deal of professional gloom
and even despair among church people, could be di-
verted into other channels. I cannot, for instance, believe that the great though perhaps overpraised ecu-
menical movement among the non-Roman churches
will move out of its present impasse—in which a due
recognition of differences is having the unfortunate
effect of leading to an intensification rather than ameli-
oration of those differences—until a profound effort
is made to recognize both the need and the proper
claims of the so-called secular humanist world. Towards the need of that world the Church has no other
task than it has always had—to serve. And towards
the claims of the world the Church is required to pay
much more attentive respect than hitherto. What I am
thinking of here is a temper as well as a quality of
mind, rather than a new set of principles: a temper and
a quality of mind which will allow the world to be itself and in loving humility to elicit from the world's
achievements and from its failures the possibilities
which might lead it farther. What is required is what
Jacques Ellul calls a 'style of life'. The Church cannot
stand over the world with a whip; nor can it get behind it with a load of dynamite. The whip and the
dynamite, where available, would be better used on
itself. The world is not, I think, 'hungry for God' in
the sense of popular conservatizing evangelists, who
really mean by that a hunger to hear their own words

in the old accepted terminology of their fathers—or rather their grandfathers (for their fathers knew better). The world is very suspicious, and rightly so, of those who cry 'The temple of the Lord are these', for it has had long experience of the unbridled ambitions of the Church over against the world. What the world would really see gladly is an honest and complete recognition, without any ulterior motives, by those who claim to carry forward the message of Christianity, of the existence of the world with all its own principles of movement, hopes and possibilities.

If I may venture a specific criticism, I should say that the Church needs not only in its practice but above all in its spiritual and intellectual pursuits in its colleges and universities, as well as in the manses and vicarages of its clergy, to be able far more thoroughly to identify itself, without reserve, with the studies and work of the world. It needs to recognize the hidden unconditional ground even in the most autonomous of human pursuits, it needs to welcome those pursuits not for the hope that they may be violently 'baptized' into Christ, but for their own sake. I would rather see more Christians devoting themselves today to some pursuit in what is commonly called the world— whether an intellectual study or a practical activity— than an increase in the numbers of theological students, however desirable that may seem for the immediate purposes and needs of the church authorities. If the unity of truth and being in Christ is more than a piece of sentimentalizing, then this identifying of one-

self fully with the things and the people in the world is
in fact an absolutely necessary step in the same direction taken by the incarnate Lord, who took upon himself the form of a servant in absolute seriousness and
not merely as a docetic whimsy.

4

SOME SOLUTIONS

So far I have been content to give you a historical survey and a cultural analysis, first in the Bible, and then in the course of Christian history, of the problem which lies at its heart, the problem which obsessed Kierkegaard and which can be summed up in his persistent question, 'How do I become a Christian?' I have shown how the Church, though it has tried different ways and faced several critical moments, did not follow out the possibilities which were opened up with the break-up of the mediaeval metaphysical domination. Today, in the midst of a world characterized by anxiety and hopelessness, we are still asking, and being asked, the same question. We are in the midst of a crisis in human history of unprecedented dimensions. How is the fundamental question, the question about God and Christ and our relation to them, being answered?

In general, I think it is true to say that the acuteness of the crisis, with its long roots back into Christian history, has not been recognized by any of the conventional groups within the Church. The assumptions made by these groups are too abstract; or they

are mere clichés; or they cling grimly to some part of
the truth, or some expression of it, which was once,
in its own time and place, urgent and operative for
history, but is now a museum piece, shabby and outmoded, because unable to work, unable to catch and
fire the imagination and the will as well as the uneasy
conscience and faltering understanding of men today.

I want first, therefore, to look at some of these
main groupings or tendencies in the Church, and
examine their relation to the present questions of
men, as well as their provenance in history. The first
main tendency I should describe as archaism. This
may take one of several different forms, but in general
it is characterized by a kind of nostalgia for some
great figure or event in the history of the group.
Among Roman Catholics and their intellectual fellow-
travellers the dominant archaism is dogmatic. Neo-
Thomism, a reiteration and re-furbishing of the dogmatic structure of St Thomas Aquinas, is claimed as
the panacea for the problems of society. With the aid
of a philosophy which was formulated in quite different conditions and for quite different ends, the
adherents of this archaism attempt to interpret the
nature and the predicament of man in this twentieth
century. In contrast with the shifting and uncertain
claims of other groups, the neo-Thomist movement
is a mighty authority. I do not need to elaborate
this by detailing its conquests of individual minds.
An interesting sociological study could be made of
the particular kinds of people who are attracted in

their adult life into the Roman communion. Undoubtedly the aesthetic grandeur of the Roman tradition is attractive, while at the same time it conceals the harsh lines of authoritarian dogma. Again, the plausible and impressive philosophy of the analogy of being serves to soften the rigid lines of thought. And thirdly, it is important to remember that the Roman Church is almost as much an ideal or a grandiose accommodating and comprehensive symbol, open and generous to all kinds of temperaments and ideas, as it is an aesthetic tradition and a dogmatic system. Its outlines may therefore easily be blurred, or may appear so remote to the individual, that he may move comfortably within the allotted space. But the space *is* an allotted one, as can well appear with sudden clarity and sharpness in any emergency of belief or of morals. The *ex cathedra* pronouncements of the papal authority in these realms are the waiting dragon to encircle and devour any overreaching freedom of the human spirit.

Therefore it is only necessary to remember that the authority which is thus set up over men's lives is in the last resort a denial of the real independence of men, their responsibility for their own destiny, and their freedom to give substance to their destiny in ever new forms of society and thought. By such a backward spring into history men are indeed invited to find rest for their minds; and within the generous confines set by the worldly authority of an authoritarian church many people do indeed find rest, and strength to achieve what they may achieve in such circumstances. But not all the grandeur and success of this movement can make up for the loss of the essential freedom of the human spirit, without which in the end the human spirit must stifle. Out of the fixed transcendent categories of Thomism, grandiose, substantial, and eternal, there flows no quickening spirit for the needs and problems of our time. Only by turning on our traces, only by being blind and deaf to the cries and questions of our fellow-men today, is it possible to imagine that we have found the absolute solution for the world in such a retrogression.

The archaism of neo-Calvinism does not have anything essentially different to offer. It too turns in romantic longing back to the great figure of its past. Its note has perhaps less of grand tragedy in it than the resolute and sustained effort of the Old Church. For though the same cardinal principle of heteronomy is at work here too—the principle, that is, of imposing an alien dogmatic system on a society which is looking in entirely different directions—the Calvinist heteronomy is no more than a shadow of the great dogmatic system of the mediaeval Church. In its deepest impulses the Reformation was never intended to mean the re-establishment of the old authority in new dress. When Luther cast aside 'holy clothes' he was doing more than divest himself of the trappings of a corrupt authority: he was acting under the impulse of that movement of the human spirit which I have called the great revolution in man's self-understanding. To attempt to identify this movement of the spirit, as neo-Calvinism does, even with a purified form of the heteronomous institution of the Church, is a fearful mutilation of the emergent new society. For it was no new dogma, not even *sola fide*, considered as a dogma of the old kind, which was the real characteristic of the Reformation. The Protestant spirit needs to be characterized rather in terms of a living encounter with the Holy Spirit, with responsibility and freedom towards and in history. Of this positive side of things I shall have more to say in my last lecture.

Another grouping may be seen today on a different basis, a narrower front, within the opposed battalions of the Church itself. This is the now well-established conflict between fundamentalism and liberalism. This has so many variations, and has now gone on for so long, that it might almost seem to be a necessity for the existence of the Church—like the battles in George Orwell's story, *Nineteen Eighty-four*, where wars went on between the great configurations of forces as a matter of policy and a matter of course. The battle within the Church circles round a very important question—namely, the question of the method by which Christian truth is expressed, handed down, and to be preached. More precisely, the question is about the authority of the Scriptures of the Old and New Testaments. The fundamentalist view clings to the doctrine of the verbal inerrancy of the whole body of Scripture. This doctrine is, of the two, the more complete and immediately satisfying.

For it makes an uncompromising demand for the sacrifice of the whole spirit of intellectual inquiry. This demand is disguised as the claim of the very Word of God upon your mind, and is mostly taken, by opponents as well as adherents, at the value it puts upon itself. In other words, if you are prepared to deliver your mind, shackled and submissive, to the claims of the Word as a vast and efficient juggernaut, then here too you are promised peace of a kind. You may even find this peace. But behind the disguise of a total submission to the Word of God there lurks in fact another man-made structure, namely, a highly selective theory of revelation, a kind of gnosticism which claims to drag down from heaven an individual experience of illumination sufficient for every situation and problem which may arise in human conduct and aspiration at any period. In this selective appropriation of 'knowledge' necessary for salvation there is implicit an absolute denial of the whole movement of the human spirit which you find displayed in such a character as Petrarch, or Francis Bacon, or Luther, or the other great lords of the Renaissance, and you will have much assurance added to your spirit. Only one thing will be lacking, your freedom as a Christian man.

And of course, you will as a result have nothing to say to those who stand outside this realm of pseudo-submission, of arrogance masquerading as obedience, or to those who are in fact pioneering in all the realms of human enterprise today. For the pre-requisite of

being able to speak to others is that you should be
with them where they are; not merely exercising
your benevolence on their need or your intelligence
on their problems; but being truly with them. This
being with others and for others, which is the substance of love, is not an individualist manœuvre,
but points rather to the grand strategy of real
historical life. If your Christian attitude is restricted
to the assertion of the self-contained truth of the
Word of God understood from within your own
situation, then it lacks this essential outgoing movement, the action of love which is poured out, not as a
pathetic spectacle but as a real encounter of being
with being. This lack, which is really a pervasive
lovelessness, is apparent in the whole fundamentalist
apprehension of the Word of God and the intention
of Christianity. The world is denied by such an apprehension. It is set at a distance, and the space between
the avowed fundamentalist Christian and the world is
not filled, as it can be, and must be, by the action of
understanding love. Those 'over there', or 'outside',
in the world, are also looking for the gifts which
Christianity has to lavish upon them. But they will
not find these gifts except in the depths of a personal
encounter which includes a being-with them in the
whole of their lives and interests.

But the solution is not to be found, either, in the
liberalism which is the conventional opponent of fundamentalism. This movement of thought can be ill-
defined, for it has ramifications far beyond the matter

of how to interpret and understand the Bible. Within the narrower theme, however, liberalism may be described as the effort to extract from the teachings of the Bible certain permanent and timeless truths which may be suitably applied to every human situation. Such truths have been taken to be, for instance, the fatherhood of God, the brotherhood of man, love of your neighbour, belief in the inevitable progress of mankind, and the like. Noble thoughts, indeed; and it would be a shoddy mind which simply laughed at the hopes and ideals of our fathers and grandfathers as these found practical expression in their actions, in politics, in economics, in the great humanitarian and missionary enterprises of last century and the first half of this century. But in the end these ideals have been found inadequate, and the practical good works which flowed directly from them have either come to an end or been assimilated to the residual activities of western civilization. The ideals were inadequate because they were abstractions from the real situation of men. They avoided the historicity of the Christian foundation; so they were not able to face and conquer the evil, or the *Angst*, or the despair, which rises up again and again in the midst of the most ideal situation. The strength of liberalism lies in its recognition of the need for Christianity to be applied to the human situation; its weakness lies in its readiness to discard or to ignore the brute historical scandal of Christianity in order the more readily to apply its tenets to society. For liberal idealism and modernism lose touch with the completeness of the Word of God. They have lost the understanding of it as a historical entity, or rather as a historical situation or event, which rises to its climax in the Incarnate Word but has also manifestations through the whole history of Israel both before and after Christ. In this regard liberalism may be justly accused of making a false and unnecessary concession to a passing phase of humanism, to that sterile and limited anthropology which sees man as completed not in history but in ideas, which sees the Word and the Spirit and God not as historical and encounterable Being but as ideas, and which presupposes and sanctions a spiritualized conception of man which has lost the historical heart of Christianity. The cross, the resurrection and the second coming become, on this view, a shadowy backcloth to an undialectic version of Christianity. The historical tragedy and the consequent seriousness and living nature of the historical triumph of God's work are submerged by an onflowing idea—whether the idea of progress, or of the common goal of all mankind in a grand amalgam of all good ideas and all goodwill which is nicknamed the kingdom of God, or the like—the interruptions to which, from sin, or evil, or death, are seen as no more than casual interruptions. This denial of the actual living historical situation in which man has to live and suffer is really a denial of the reality of man's being as a historical creature, and it bears, incidentally, an ominous resemblance to the Marxist philosophy of the relation of the individual to the idea—which springs of course, from the same idealist seed-bed. In a word, liberalism ends by losing both itself and the Christianity it seeks to serve.

*

All these proposed remedies—archaism, heteronomism, fundamentalism, liberalism—come to grief because they are based on a partial or distorted understanding of what has been happening to man during the centuries of the modern world. They have their partial and temporary successes because men are often happy to find relief from their pain by any means that lies to hand. When the pain goes as deep as it does today, it is not surprising that a loud voice, or the panoply of authority, can provide the illusion of a real conversion, a turning in the right direction. The shores of the Christian world are littered with the hulks or the jetsam of false loyalties, which have led only to rack and ruin. These illusory invitations are not the only ones to attract people today. A political party, a mass movement, even music, may provide the temporary illusion of an entry into an absolute world. But they are all alike illusory, because they ignore the one inescapable human element, that which makes a man truly human—his personal responsibility—and with bland cruelty they expose what is left of a man, after such a conversion, as another 'head', another number, a swelling of their statistics, a new recruit for their battle against—one another. Or the result may be the very opposite of the false comfort of being lost

in a marching herd: it can happen that a man who has
sought his assurance, and the truth of his life, in one
such grouping will fail to find it and will be left
more alone than ever.

It is important to look at this situation of man today
with unclouded eyes. Perhaps Martin Buber, the
Jewish philosopher, has made the clearest and most
disturbing diagnosis of our state, particularly in his
early work *I and Thou*, first published in German as
long ago as 1923, and in the later sequel to it published in English in 1947 with the title *Between Man
and Man*. In these works he elaborates the two-fold
nature of all human life in what he calls an I-It and
an I-Thou relation. It is the I-It relation which is
dominant in every sphere today; not only in those
spheres where it is properly and legitimately active,
in experiences of using and enjoying, of handling and
examining, but also in the spheres where the I-Thou
relation should really hold sway, above all in the relations between men. As a result of the failure of the
I-Thou relation there has been a loss of the personal,
the truly human, throughout the whole world of human activities, and what is left is the alternative,
collectivism or individualism. Massification, or isolation: that is the common choice which lies before most
people today. Either you walk in step with the rest,
doing the things they do, thinking and feeling as they
do, and so lose your personal responsibility. Or you
rebel, and break free, and enter into isolation. Here
too your responsibility withers, for you can be

F   [81]

responsible only along with others. Community is the being together of persons in responsible action. But neither collectivism nor individualism permits this kind of responsibility. Collective man is the man without a face, with only a number. He is not a separate responsible person, making his own choices and decisions, he does not meet others in the strength of his own will, and out of the depth of his own being. He has in fact no being of his own, but only illusory being, the chimera of being which he borrows like a cloak from his fellows in the collective. His sign in fact is that cloak or uniform of the collective, and uniformity is the fulfilment at which he aims. Sometimes such a man responds to the despair within himself, or to a call from outside himself, and seeks to escape from the marching herd; he seeks for himself a name and a face. But if he is not ready to enter without reserve into that relation of responsibility which in its highest reaches is characterized by the grave words, 'to love another', then all he is able to find outside himself is—himself. In other words, he is sunk into a more profound isolation than ever, the isolation of the poetic Narcissus, admiring his own image in a pool of water, or the isolation of the philosophic solipsist, finding existence only in himself. He has escaped from the prison of the collective into the romantic tower of his own self.

If these are terrible and searching thoughts when applied to the generality of men today, they become even more terrible when applied to the would-be community of Christians. The consequences are more terrible where the claims are so high. In the sphere of the state, of politics or economics, where a collective or an individual becomes too powerful, or evil, or runs amok, he can still be restrained by war or some other exercise of force, bound and fettered, and put away. But what can you do with a Church that has lost the life of community? It is bad enough if such an organization depends on one of these theological or ritual tendencies, which I have already described, as the explanation and justification of its existence. But it is infinitely worse if such an organization imagines that it thereby possesses community, being-together, *koinonia*. Here you expect to see the fulfilment of human possibilities: people who have come to themselves in the only true way—living, that is, no longer for themselves but for others, within the objective structure of grace. I do not say they live as saints; nor should one distort the issue by demanding that they be born again in the strict evangelical connotation of recent generations. But they must live in openness and expectation of the possibility of being, in an emerging new community. That is, they must live as persons, and not as faceless numbers or as solipsists recognizing no other existences; they must live with and for one another in the extremity of responsible care which is called love.

Has the Church any awareness of its plight? Is there any point where it is trying to communicate, even within its own body, to the breaking-off and

dying members? I do not think that the true note of
evangelism is being sounded, or that the invitation to
life in community is being offered, at any of the points
I have described. Nor is it being truly offered in the
mass movements of so-called revival which are a
marked feature of church life in many places today.
The work of the Oxford Groups, or Moral Re-
Armament, and the work of Dr Billy Graham, are two
examples of this kind of effort. Graham's work is
hopelessly constricted to a would-be biblical view of
life, which combines a kind of naïve biblicism with an
evangelical pietism of the nineteenth century brand,
and cannot even envisage the problems of modern
man in the death-grip of his false communities. And
Moral Re-Armament, which has a longer and more
varied record of successes to its credit, is unable to
penetrate to the heart of man's position and need today—for so many different reasons that I hardly think
it worthwhile attempting to list them. At bottom,
Moral Re-Armament, though vividly aware of the
deficiencies of the conventional church forms, is itself
unable to offer more than a kind of personalist apprehension of certain conventional formulas of old-
fashioned evangelism; for here too the biblical apprehension lacks flexibility and depth and range sufficient
to turn the history of men in a new direction. Conversion of the classic kind—such as you see at work
in men like Moses, and Jeremiah, and Paul, and
Augustine—has always meant a new direction for history, conquest of whole new areas for the structure of

grace, and a quickened apprehension of the total claim made by the sovereign Lord of history on the historical life of men in society. Such fashionable and even successful movements cannot give us our answer. For they do not disclose an absolute relation to history, they do not lift a man out of the collective or out of his individualism into that free spontaneous and creative life where he can live in the Spirit. They fix men, they do not free them. They bind them to loyalty to a cause, or to a catchword; they smother them in emotions, or swaddle them in old forms. Movements of that kind should be measured not by their success in collecting scalps—I have never heard that the Church should be a kind of scalp-hunter—but by their relation to the total historical possibilities of Christianity in meeting other people, in the place where they are, in all their ambiguity, with an absolute demand for wholeness and love.

One of the points where I do see hope, where that absolute demand begins to be heard, lies in the work of the German scholar Rudolf Bultmann. This New Testament scholar has spent the whole of his life in the examination and interpretation of the New Testament writings. In the course of his work he has set many a cat among many pigeons. He was one of the founders of the form-critical method of analysing and dissecting the Gospels in an effort to recover the genuine sayings lying a generation behind the written tradition of the Church, which is what we possess in our written Gospels. In recent years he has started a fire which promises to become a conflagration. His own Church seriously considered whether he should not be arraigned for heresy. His concern has been quite simple : it is to find a way of interpreting and stating the gospel that is apprehensible to modern people. His presupposition, of course, is immense : it is that in fact the gospel is incomprehensible to typical modern people. He would, I think, subscribe to the analysis, at least in its broad outlines, which I have been giving you of the predicament in which we have found ourselves since the Renaissance. I mean that he would acknowledge as his presupposition (as it is mine) that a new way of looking at man, and a new conception of man's place in history and responsibility for history, arose with the overthrow of mediaeval civilization. Man ceased to be bound to a specific metaphysic, and was made ready for a new inner-worldly freedom and responsibility which have led him away from the mythological and eschatological world view presupposed in the New Testament. In other words, Bultmann sees a new man in being, or in process of being, in becoming, a man with still nothing more than inchoate form, with only the faint outlines of a face and a form—like those great unfinished figures of Michelangelo struggling out of the hard stone from which he intended to shape them. Bultmann is in fact concerned with the clear and conscious emergence of a new possibility in man. In this respect his work demands, what it has not yet received, to be studied in conjunction with the breakdown of old forms in art and letters, in music and writing and painting. The connexion is not a mere coincidence, but indicates a general sense, among the seers and makers, of the new world which is possibly just over the horizon, just round the corner. You may recall how Archbishop Søderblom once defined the Christian apprehension of the kingdom of God as being 'always just round the corner'. It is in this kind of existentialist sense that the vivid potentialities of man can regain their eschatological potency. For Bultmann, though he is ruthless with the primitive Jewish eschatology which controls a great deal of the mode of expression of the New Testament, is by no means a liberal who wants to get rid of eschatology. On the contrary, he wishes to restore to Christian life an existentialist eschatology as a force striking out of our future into our present.

A great cry has been raised against his views, echoing from every quarter. There are those who call him an old-fashioned liberal in theology, who merely wants to extract and accommodate the essence of the gospel to passing fashions. There are those who say that by wanting to free the gospel message from its mythological and apocalyptic forms he is attempting the impossible, for the truths of religion must always be clothed in symbols and myths. There are those who say that at all times the gospel has been a scandal to natural man, and Bultmann is simply trying to remove the scandal. In the context of these lectures I would rather say that in Bultmann we find the effort to restate a doctrine of man which will bear equally upon

[87]

the churched and the unchurched, on the rump of the
Christian world and upon its needy successors, the
humanists. He is calling for a radical re-interpretation
of the whole body of traditional Christian theology.
One thing he is clearly not doing, and that is abandon-
ing the scandal of the historicity and particularity of
the Incarnation. Though he finds much in the Gospels
which is meaningless and pointless in its present form,
since it depends on primitive Jewish apocalyptic or on
first-century gnosticism, he does not thereby throw
overboard the substance of the *kerygma*. He still asks,
with extreme urgency, the burning question, how do
I become a Christian. It is the history, and the historicity, which he wants to recover, not as the quintess-
ence of an idealist philosophy, not as a body of alien
dogma to be imposed on modern men, with that kind
of positivism which says 'Take it or leave it', and not
even as a kind of private experience either of the
'numinous' or of outright dependence. Neither Bar-
thianism nor a 'simple' experiential faith of the
Schleiermacher-Otto tradition provides, on Bultmann's view, a sufficient understanding either of the
historical being of Christianity or of the individual's
own being. Bultmann wants to recover the history as
a living relation of his being to the structure of grace.
'Faith', he says, 'is the answer to the question of the
kerygma which continually addresses me', and it is
this *kerygma* which he wishes to uncover in its own
life and legitimacy from the mists and twists which it
has suffered through one form or another of meta-

physical or idealist imposition. It has of course been objected that Bultmann has only replaced one philosophy by another, and that the existentialist philosophy. For it is with the aid of existentialist analysis, in particular that of Heidegger, that he presents his view of man in his natural state. But this analysis, as he himself clearly says, is a descriptive or phenomenological analysis which merely brings us to the threshold: it brings us towards the *kerygma* without pretensions. It is in that situation that it first becomes possible for men really to face the question in the *kerygma* of the historical existence of Jesus.

So far as there is one problem in what I have been saying, we have touched upon it here. It is the problem of the relation of faith to history. When I am invited to believe the gospel, a whole host of problems arises; but chief is this strange question about how it is possible to be related in faith to events which are sunk in the past. This is not merely a question of memory or of certain fixed data, such as knowing that Caesar was murdered, or that William the Conqueror won the battle of Hastings. Both these important events are important because they have a certain effect on our lives, even today, shaping their form and even their content in certain respects whether we know about these events or not. But the relation with the historical events of the life of Jesus is different, for here I am asked to believe that my eternal happiness is at stake. Many answers have been attempted to this question, and to look at them would take us far into

the history of religions as well as into the history of
Christian dogma. But the guiding clue through the
labyrinth seems to me to lie for our day in the hands
of Bultmann, when he disentangles from the events an
element of transcendence which is not the transcendence of merely wonderful happenings, not the transcendence of a primitive mythology of heaven and
earth, not the transcendence expressed in gnosticism
(which is no more than an extension of the world,
without the conception of a Creator), and not the
transcendence expressed in primitive eschatology. But
the transcendence which he perceives in the Christ-
event is a transcendence which shines through history,
where grace springs up as it were in the midst of human life, where responsibility is absolute, where the
individual is invited to decide towards an objective
possibility of grace. This is the kind of conversion
which lifts the subject out of himself, out of his fears
and his sins, into a forgiven life. Thenceforth he is
open to the world and to others, he is at peace. He is
no longer confident in himself, boasting in the flesh;
but his confidence is in the eternal Thou who is present through the given Word, recurrent in each personal situation of responsibility. This is the meeting
of man with God which takes place, in faithful response, in human history. This is neither a metaphysical assertion about God's attributes, nor an emotional
excitation in face of the unknowable Eternal. 'To
know Christ is to know his benefits', said the young
Melanchthon; and 'we cannot know God as he is, but

only in what he does to us', said Wilhelm Herrmann, Bultmann's own teacher in Marburg. In the day-to-day decisions of the responsible person, in every sphere with which he has to do, this absolute meeting may be disclosed. It is not an extra to those day-to-day events, but appears in and through them. It is truer to say that God is met through the world than over and above it. He comes not 'plumb down from above', but is to be glimpsed in every event, in every needy hand upraised, every conflict of will, every utterance of hope or love. This relation of faith to history, then, is made possible by the initiating action of God's grace throughout history; in the Incarnate Word supremely, but not there alone. This Word comes to us out of history because it comes to us now, in our present. Past history is real, and related to us, because it is not past, but present.

Further, this presence of past history, this true historism is filled out and confirmed not by the past alone, but by the potentialities contained in the past, i.e., by the future. The potentialities of the Word are boundless, but they are not vague. They are explicitly and clearly contained within human history. That is to say, past and future combine in the present. The Incarnate Word is focused ever anew in the present history of man. The future is as important as the past. The mythology of the second coming is intended to tell us something not about some ineffable cosmic conclusion, some supra-historical and therefore un-historical end to history, but about the fulness of

history itself. What began as history, and has meaning
as present history, cannot end as anything but history
without emptying the reality out of the whole of
history, and therefore, of course, out of the historical
Incarnation as the concentrated climax of God's
speech with men. Again and again we find that the
drift, the temptation, the easy way out, for Christian
faith is towards the denial of the historicity of faith
as the supreme moment towards which God is
inviting his world. But the Lord of history who will
come again will not destroy history, nor will he
cap it with something incomprehensible to and different from history. The faith in him who will come
again is an indissoluble part of the historicity of God's
purpose. Man is not meant to be cast down by the
awful premonition of the trumpet of the Lord sounding in his ears. Rather he is intended to hear it as a
clarion call rising out of the triumph of God within
history. This triumph has already been achieved.
Only its celebration awaits us. In this sense the second
coming is not different from the first coming. To con-
tinue the mythological idiom, the trumpet is sounding
to the ears of faith in every present situation, putting
a period to history, indeed, but thereby making and
not destroying that history. So we may legitimately
speak of the future being contained in the past, the
second coming in the first coming, and all history
lying open before us. It is in this confidence that the
Christian can see man rising to new heights over and
beyond the dark valleys of sin and despair and death,

by which he believes himself today (as every man in his own day) to be specially tempted. Confidence is available to the man who lives by faith so far as he lives in and through the forgiveness offered to him by God's dealing with all history, past, present and future, and so far as he lives, in consequence, with an open mind, free for his responsibilities, open and free towards all that may come. This is the eschatology which releases us from bondage to a mythology, and proleptically brings before us, in our present commitments, all the glory and certainty of the end. It is a historical end, that is all we can say about it. We cannot predict its form, we cannot imagine its nature. History is full of surprises, for it is the conspiracy, the public covenant, between God and man; and neither man nor God is fettered. In the freedom of the invitation and the freedom of the response history moves freely towards its unimagined goal.

It is in the setting of this kind of faith that we have to consider still the positive possibilities open to us in our present history, and these I hope to suggest in my concluding lecture.

5

THIS-WORLDLY TRANSCENDENCE

IN this lecture I want to indicate what seems to me to be the way through the impasse for proper belief—a way which leads ultimately, of course, to practical demands and consequences for Christian action. Here, however, I am concerned only with the presuppositions of a new theology of man which may be adequate to what I believe to be the immense future still awaiting our society if it can come to a proper understanding of itself.

So far I have been talking of failures: the failure of the Renaissance, and the failure of the Reformation. The Renaissance failed to follow out the logic of its own maturity by means of a full doctrine of man; and the Reformation failed to apprehend the full freedom offered to it by the breaking of the mediaeval metaphysical bonds. There has been a series of attempts to fight for a solution, but in the main the heirs of the Renaissance have worked on without hope, and the heirs of the Reformation have proposed solutions which have been little more than rearguard actions in defence of untenable positions. The gulf between the conventional Christian position and the position of

ordinary unchurched men has been traversed by Bultmann, in the effort at demythologizing which I
sketched last time. But in the main this effort has not
been acceptable to the churches. His traversal has
been solitary, precarious, and no more accessible to
an ordinary man than, say, the first flight across the
Channel by Blériot was repeatable by any Tom, Dick
or Harry. With time and labour this pioneer effort
will work its way into the tradition, but not yet, and
not easily. Meantime, the characteristic position of
ordinary men is either that they are bundled together
in some kind of collective, or that they are isolated in
a kind of individualism which offers no hope of community. In either case community is hardly known.
Even friendship, or love, which are the high points of
real community between persons, seems to be increasingly rare.

What of the Christian in all this? What are his real
commitments and obligations? Where is his community, the Church, the new creation? And if I ask
the most urgent and personal question of all, 'What
must I do to be saved?', I intend no blasphemy or ultimate scepticism when I say that the answer given to
the jailer's question in the Book of Acts, 'Believe on
the Lord Jesus Christ', does not answer my question,
today, in my circumstances—the historical circumstances I have described—directly or satisfactorily. It
leaves me, and my companions in this modern world,
both those within and those outside the Church, with
many questions, the question about the nature of

belief, the question about who Jesus is, and where, and how, and the question about the substance of salvation itself. In other words, a great deal of re-thinking requires to be done which will be neither biblical theology by itself nor systematic theology by itself, but an existential assessment of the Bible and the world which will uncover the almost entirely dissipated claim of real transcendence as an existent force *within* this world.

One of the most illuminating entries into this whole complex of questions has been made by one whose early death was one of the most tragic losses to the Church in our time. Indeed, if I were to single out any writer from the many to whom I owe so much for these lectures, it would be he. Dietrich Bonhoeffer was a pastor of the Confessing Church in Germany who was imprisoned by the Nazis for alleged treasonable activities. The failure of the plot against Hitler's life in July 1944 led to his execution a few days before his prison was reached and opened by the advancing American troops. In the long months he spent in prison he was able to write letters, both to his parents and to a friend, some of which were preserved and later published. They have appeared in English with the title *Letters and Papers from Prison*. In these letters and fragments you see a fine, cultured, sensitive mind, heir of all the wealth of Europe, rejoicing in its treasures, but at the same time intensely concerned with the problem of the right way through for modern man to his proper life as the heir of Christianity. How to become a Christian was Bonhoeffer's

problem, as it was Kierkegaard's. There is one little
section in this volume of fragments and teasing hints
which bears the simple title 'Outline for a Book'.
Bonhoeffer says in three pages more than most men
might say in 300 pages. He sketches the plan for a
book of three chapters. The first chapter was to deal
with the coming of age of humanity, the parallel
decay of religion, and the failure, in the last analysis,
of the Protestant churches, and even of the great
battling Confessing Church during the Nazi régime in
Germany. The second chapter was to draw out the
real meaning of the Christian faith in terms of the
significant heading 'Worldliness and God': what we
mean by God, and the consequent re-interpretation of
biblical terminology, of the cultus, and the creeds. The
last chapter was to draw out the consequences for the
actual existing Church. I quote now from that short
last chapter:

'The Church is her true self only when she exists for humanity. As a fresh start she should give away all her en-
dowments to the poor and needy. The clergy should live
on the free-will offerings of their congregations, or possibly
engage in some secular calling. She must take her part in
the social life of the world, not lording it over men, but
helping and serving them.'

I do not think that Bonhoeffer is merely repeating
here familiar exhortations to piety and good works.
He is certainly not indifferent to the power of concrete
example, drawing this as he does direct from its
source in the humanity of Jesus. But the clue to his

revolutionary thought is to be found in his fresh understanding of two things, the world and God. He does not think of these as separate entities of such a kind that you might possess and use your separate apprehension of God for a suitable assault upon the world. He says explicitly, in this same 'Outline for a Book', that the experience of transcendence is to be found in 'the concern of Jesus for others'. In other words, the transcendent is met in the solicitude for others as given to us in the life and way of Jesus. This has also an important negative implication, namely, that God is not to be met primarily in some assertion about him. God is not to be found in an abstract belief about his omnipotence, or omniscience, or even in the idea of love. God is not the idea we have of him. He is not any idea. To attempt to elevate some idea to the place of God is to make an idol and worship that instead of God. When we set up some abstraction in place of God we are worshipping nothing more than an extension of the world. This kind of false worship has led to all kinds of perversions in the history of the Church, which has always been too ready to act on behalf of God, assuming a familiarity with God which has led it to the ultimate blasphemy of killing men in the name of God and his love.

This is a moral failure. But this confusion between God and our dogmatic assertions about him has led to an intellectual as well as a moral failure. We have been all too ready, especially since the great break through of the Renaissance, to fight a kind of battle

against the world on behalf of God. Here too the
Church has desired, as it were, to rescue God from
the consequences of his own recklessness first in
creating and then in saving his world. God's liberating action in his Word—which as I have repeatedly
said can be seen as truly liberating only when it is
seen as more than an isolated occurrence in history—
has been disallowed by the common-sense of Christian
people as altogether too dashing, too audacious and
foolhardy. So when the break through of man's spirit
beat back the Christian warrior from one entrenched
position after another, the Christian response in recent
centuries has varied little. Before the advancing battalions of intelligence and reason and scepticism, as
one area of knowledge after another was captured for
technology, or science, or psychology, God has been
rescued by too willing hands. The children of light
have been happily engaged in drawing God back into
the darkness, beyond the frontiers of assured life, into
the region which is euphemistically called the mystery
of God. The mystery of God has been equated with a
kind of *terra incognita*, an as-yet unknowable rather
than as a truly ineffable mystery, which is to say a
present mystery whose mystery is an actual, encountered, lived experience of an incomprehensible
but not inapprehensible gift. The consequences of this
series of retreats have been distortion of the understanding of God, confusion among the ranks on both
sides, and dishonour of God's name. For in fact by
thus attempting to safeguard God, the Church has

[99]

only been safeguarding its idea of God. It has been honouring not the incarnate Word in the bleeding helplessness of utter service, but an emasculated Jesus, the Jesus of the *Ersatz* gold halo and the tawdry pietism of decadent Jesusology. It has been honouring not the God in the midst of the world but a kind of escape mechanism devised by its own fears. In one magnificent letter, written while bombing raids were being carried out over his prison, Bonhoeffer sums up the confusion of the Church in our time in these words:

'While I often shrink with religious people from speaking of God by name—because that name somehow here seems to me not to ring true, and I strike myself as rather dishonest (it is especially bad when others start talking in religious jargon: then I dry up completely and feel somehow oppressed and ill at ease)—with the people who have no religion I am able on occasion to speak of God quite openly and as it were naturally. Religious people speak of God when human perception is (often just from laziness) at an end, or human resources fail: it is really always the *deus ex machina* they call to their aid, either for the so-called solving of insoluble problems or as support in human failure—always, that is to say, helping out human weakness or on the borders of human existence. Of necessity, that can only go on until men can, by their own strength, push those borders back a little further, so that God becomes superfluous as a *deus ex machina*. I have come to be doubtful even about talking of "borders of human existence". Is even death today, since men are scarcely afraid of it any more, and sin, which they scarcely understand any more, still a genuine border-line? It always seems to me that in

talking thus we are only seeking frantically to make room
for God. I should like to speak of God not on the borders
of life but at its centre, not in weakness but in strength, not,
therefore, in man's suffering and death but in his life and
prosperity. On the borders it seems to me better to hold
our peace and leave the problem unsolved . . . God is the
"beyond" in the midst of our life. The Church stands not
where human powers give out, on the borders, but in the
centre of the village.'[1]

This powerful recognition of the place of God in his
world springs from Bonhoeffer's understanding of the
nature of the encounter with Jesus. 'Faith', he says,
'is participation in this being of Jesus (incarnation, cross, and resurrection). Our relationship to God
is not a religious relationship to a supreme being,
absolute in power and goodness, which is a spurious
conception of transcendence, but a new life for others,
through participation in the being of God. The transcendence consists not in tasks beyond our scope, but
in the thing nearest to hand. God in human form, not,
as in other religions, in animal form—the monstrous,
chaotic, remote and terrifying—nor yet in abstract
form—the absolute, metaphysical, infinite, etc.—nor
yet in the Greek divine-human of autonomous
man, but man existing for others, and hence the Cru-
cified. A life based on the transcendent'.[2]

This understanding of the encounter with Jesus
proposes a dialectic of transcendence which can, I

[1]Op. cit., 124.
[2]Op. cit., 179.

think, lead us through our modern impasse. On the one hand there is here a recognition of the status of the world as the place to which Jesus came, the place where he was Jesus, and as a consequence of which he is what he is. This leads Bonhoeffer to his repeated but alas not fully elaborated remarks about what he calls worldliness or religionlessness. In one letter he says:

'The thing that keeps coming back to me is, what *is* Christianity, and indeed what *is* Christ, for us today? The time when men could be told everything by means of words, whether theological or simply pious, is over, and so is the time of inwardness and conscience, which is to say the time of religion as such. We are proceeding towards a time of no religion at all: men as they now are simply cannot be religious any more. Even those who honestly describe themselves as "religious" do not in the least act up to it, and so when they say "religious" they evidently mean something quite different. Our whole nineteen-hundred-year-old Christian preaching and theology rests upon the "religious premise" of man. What we call Christianity has always been a pattern—perhaps a true pattern—of religion. But if one day it becomes apparent that this *a priori* premise simply does not exist, but was an historical and temporary form of human self-expression, i.e. if we reach the stage of being radically without religion—and I think this is more or less the case already, else how is it, for instance, that this war is not calling forth any "religious" reaction—what does that mean for Christianity? . . . How can Christ become the Lord even of those with no religion? If religion is no more than the garment of Christianity—and even that garment has had very different aspects at different periods—then what is a religionless Christianity? . . . What is the significance of a Church . . . in a religionless world? How do we speak of God without religion? . . . In what way are we in a religionless and secular sense Christians . . . not conceiving of ourselves religiously as specially favoured, but as wholly belonging to the world? Then Christ is no longer an object of religion, but something quite different, indeed and in truth the Lord of the world.'[1]

I am quite sure that in such letters Bonhoeffer was breaking through to a fresh apprehension of the status of man and the world as something existing in their own right as the place where God loves to be. You might say that he was reaching a new apprehension of the meaning of this world, and ourselves, as creation, as creatures; but it was not an abstract or isolated apprehension, but closely connected, indeed flowing out of, his apprehension of Christ as Lord of the world. That, at least, seems to have been the intention of the remarks he has made in such letters, though in fact it is not so easy to see how he could, out of such views, ever have constructed an orthodox doctrine of the relation of Christ to the Father.

The important point for our thoughts, however, is the tension between this affirmation about man and the world, about man's worldliness and religionlessness, and the other side of Bonhoeffer's position. It is this other side which holds Bonhoeffer from

[1]Op. cit., 122–3.

degenerating into a stoic position about the world in its
self-sufficiency. He calls it *Arkandisziplin*, arcane or
secret discipline. This is the heart of his thought, but
it would be wrong to think of it as a kind of individualist retreat, a kind of cultivation of inwardness or even
a search for personal salvation. He rightly points out
that in the Old Testament there is really nothing said
about saving one's soul, and in the New Testament
the focus of everything is righteousness and the kingdom of God. 'It is not', he writes, 'with the next
world that we are concerned, but with this world as
created and preserved and set subject to laws and
atoned for and made new.' What sustains him is nothing very original, but it is the climax as well as the
ground of all his belief. It is a kind of humorous,
humble, self-effacing secrecy of devotion and hope,
which finds no counterpart in the visible world, nothing in symbol or gesture by which it may be fully
reflected and expressed; nothing in the cult or the
ritual which may presume to take its place. I do
not mean that Bonhoeffer denied or decried the place
of symbol and gesture and ritual; only they were
secondary, part of that special development of re-
sponses and expressions of faith which are summed up
as 'religion'. Bonhoeffer was looking past these
things to the form for his faith which actually could
meet the world, actually be in it, without reserve, as
Christ was in it. He would have quoted with approval
the saying of Tillich that Jesus came in order to destroy religion. That faith itself rested on the sketchy

and strange tradition within Christianity of secrecy, exclusiveness, fastidiousness, which has never received great prominence. (Of modern writings I know only a letter of von Hügel, that great Catholic Christian, on the express theme of fastidiousness.) It is the tradition whose origins lie in the same region as the origins of the doctrine of election; but it has a different bent and outcome. 'Cast not your pearls before swine'; 'shake off the dust of that city from your feet'; 'this is my body': these are all sayings which presuppose, indeed demand, a kind of initiation and secrecy which clearly forbids the intrusion of the curious or the self-certain. The words of Christ are for all, indeed, and the powerful strain of universalism has swept Christianity along many triumphant lines. Paul's equally powerful stress on the givenness, the gift, of God's grace, combines with this universalism to keep the idea of secrecy and exclusiveness from too great prominence in Christian history. Nevertheless it is there, and the simplicities of the gospel, the call to be humble, and unostentatious in prayer, never using naked power, but always service, and sacrifice, are both its sustenance and its preservative.

The real strength and significance of this secret discipline, however, is its persistent pushing of the believer back into the world. He may not escape, as Reinhold Niebuhr once remarked that theological students tend to do, when they are faced with an insoluble problem: by quitting grappling, and taking an elevator to the eternal. The Christian discipline does not permit such an escape, for it is not really interested in such a conception of the eternal at all.

These two elements, then, the worldliness of God and the secret discipline, come together in a powerful dialectic in Bonhoeffer's thought. The Christian will remain in the tension of this dialectic all his days. Any interpretation of the Christian dialectic in other terms, such as the tension of the kingdom that is realized and the kingdom that is still to come, or the tension of this world and the next, of earth and heaven, rests upon a too narrow conception of eschatology or a too naïve acceptance of the old mythology. The real dialectic, as Bonhoeffer has sketched it, does not find God in the cult, taken by itself; nor in any form of pietism or socialism, which are just two forms of escape from one side or the other of the dialectic. But this dialectic of commitment to the world demands complete responsibility in and for the world, in all its interests and problems.

Of course there are perils here, on the one hand the peril of irresponsible acquiescence in the way of the world as a self-sufficient entity, and on the other hand the peril of complete invisibility, of the practical non-existence of the secret discipline. It is hard for faith to stand the strain of a profession whose perfection consists in its not professing itself, or rather, which confirms its reality not by assertion but by submission, not by taking over the world, but by identifying itself with the world, not by resting content with just crying 'Lord, Lord', but by living in and for the same world

which has now been reconciled. But this is the necessary dialectic. You are both for the world, with all the
strength of the given situation, and against it; against
it not as an intellectual rationalization of inaction and
absolute denial of the world, but against it in the depth
of this existential dialectic. The Christian cannot be
indifferent to this world which God made and loves.
Yet how can he be other than against it in its evil and
sin and hopelessness? Both positions are necessary, and
both at the same time, and without reserve. This is the
depth and inwardness of the affliction with which Christ
was afflicted; more, it is the filling up of what is lacking
in that affliction with the whole joyous agony of the
historical failure and the historical possibilities of man.

The question which arises most acutely within this
dialectic is whether there is any room left for positive
evangelism. Does the evangelist not bring a message
with authority? Does he not proclaim, like a herald,
the message of his Lord? This is so. But the form we
are bound to give the question is just this: whether
the real evangelism in our day is not rather that kind
of identification with the world in its griefs and joys
and achievements and self-questionings—in other
words, in the maturity of the world in its self-understanding, as Bonhoeffer puts it—than the imposition
of a foreign body of traditional concepts upon that
world. To help the world to come to itself, rather than
to attempt to shake it out of itself—is that not what
has happened at the great turning-points of history?
St Augustine's theology for instance, which shaped a

thousand years of Christian history, sprang from the very situation in which he was placed, with Rome fallen and the barbarians at the gates. He could not save his diocese, or his land; but out of his work the new Christendom of the West arose.

In our situation today we cannot command the same solutions. In particular, we cannot simply bring in the mythological or the metaphysical views of transcendence with their basic premise of the religiousness of man. This does not mean that we have to abandon a doctrine of the Word of God; but it does mean that we seek another way of expressing our encounter with the majesty of the sovereign Lord of history. For the old doctrine, based on a metaphysic of distinction between the place of God and the place of man, has sunk until the effort to assert the majestic otherness of God has become merely an ineffective way of asserting man's own imprisonment within the world. The old doctrine of transcendence is nothing more than an assertion of an outmoded view of the world. The enormity of God's action in giving himself to the world in the Incarnation is no longer properly apprehended in the old way of thinking. The doctrine of the Word degenerates into pietist Jesusology or into a frantic greed to possess and manage the Word. Either way the world is not taken in full seriousness. But in the Incarnation God has affirmed the world, and affirmed history, and the particularity of history, in such a way that it is simply impossible to confine our apprehension of him to a metaphysical elaboration of the event

of the Incarnation. The power of that event can be
properly faced only in the logic of that event itself.
Some way of meeting that event without reserve and
without reduction has to be found. We call the way of
meeting and accepting it *faith*. But again, this is not
a relation to some otherwise inconceivable transcendence; it is not the so-called mystical apprehension of
the unknowable. But this relation of faith finds its
room within the sphere of historical human activity
and nowhere else. And I mean by that sphere the
whole sphere of human activity, in which the religious
element is only a part, and if my diagnosis is right a
diminishing part. I should say, to take an extreme and
provocative example, that we must be ready to take
quite seriously even the implications of an avowed
atheist like Feuerbach in his momentous wrestling
with the problem of God's being and human existence.
I quote a few sentences from his early work on *The
Essence of Christianity* : Feuerbach in this passage was
particularly concerned to disprove the need for be-
lieving in God as a special existence, with special
proofs for his existence provided in the form of
miracles and other special effects, and to that extent,
of course, he was engaging in the old discussion of
the *Aufklärung* for and against special revelation. But
in the drift of his thought I believe he was not far off
from that fresh understanding of transcendence which
I have been bringing to your attention. He writes:

'The belief in the existence of God is the belief in a special
existence, separate from the existence of man and of nature.

A special existence can only be proved in a special manner. This faith is therefore only then a true and living one when special effects, immediate appearances of God, miracles, are believed in. Where, on the other hand, the belief in God is identified with belief in the world, where the belief in God is no longer a special faith, where the general being of the world takes possession of the whole man, there vanishes also the belief in special effects and appearances of God. Belief in God is wrecked, stranded on the belief in the world, in natural effects as the only true ones. As here the belief in miracles is no longer anything more than the belief in historical, past miracles, so the existence of God is also only an historical, in itself atheistic conception'.[1]

If you have followed me so far, then you will see that the interesting thing about this argument of Feuerbach's is that he is pleading against the old arguments about the transcendent power of God for what he calls a historical existence of God. That he identifies this 'historical' with 'atheistic' is, I think, an unnecessary deviation from his own argument. A faith which takes us not out of this world, into a sphere of arbitrary interventions, but deeper into the world in its historicity, is, it seems to me, the very crux of our belief in the historical Incarnation. In this historical Word of God we see nothing arbitrary, but the endless pressure of God through the events, the things and the people and the situations, of his world. We cannot be in a closer relation to God than the one he himself provides by means of his own modest pres-

[1] E.T. of 2nd edition, 1843, 202.

sure upon us. I can quote Luther here, as Feuerbach also does in that same argument, who said:

'We have as yet so to do with God as with one hidden from us, and it is not possible that in this life we should hold communion with him face to face. All creatures are now nothing else than vain masks, under which God conceals himself, and by which he deals with us.'[1]

'As yet', says Luther, and 'vain masks'; thereby he shows the longing of the Christian for the ultimate meeting, face to face, for the blessed vision. But it is possible to hold this belief as an originating power for our faith, without our needing to inquire further into it, far less to raise a new structure of ideas to try and explain the life beyond death. Here in this life, as Luther with all his transcendental reservations clearly sees, God deals with us by and through the other creatures. This is the way in which an understanding of transcendence can come alive in our faith: within the manifold forms of God's creation and creativity his Word recurs, in our present being. God is met in his works and gifts, not in himself, and not in an idea of him. He is met at the luminous point of human existence, where the individual faces him in utter openness, receives forgiveness, and is made free.

But this facing of God is always in and through, and not other than or additional to, the facing of other people in the emergent community with them. The eternal is in time, heaven is through earth, the supernatural not other than the natural, the spiritual not

[1]Ibid., 189, note.

more than the wholly human: all these categories dissolve in the power of the one real relation, the twofold relation to people and things. Here is the real place where man is made new. The new man is man in community with man in the strength of the given grace which meets him as tasks and responsibilities and opening freedoms in actual situations in their wholeness.

This is the real hope for the world. The hope for the Church, the hope for Christendom are secondary matters. We may hope that out of the living encounter with God, within the structure of grace, of the given situation, the tenuous, fragmentary web which holds together in the delicate bonds of responsible freedom all those who are turned out from themselves, into the needs and enterprises of the world—we may hope that out of this encounter new history may be made.

It is out of such turning, such returns into the freedom offered to us, that history has always been made. It is unpredictable, surprising, having effects beyond calculation or expectation. For this encounter is the burning point, the crux, the one truly live point in the whole story of mankind: the point where a man, in the full depth of his humanity, with the whole burden of his memories which we call culture and the whole burden of his failures and sin, takes to himself, in his whole life, the words of forgiveness and the invitation to faith which are the palimpsest of all the pages of history.

INDEXES

INDEX OF NAMES

INDEX OF SUBJECTS